Patsy Doll Family Encyclopedia
Volume I

by Patricia N. Schoonmaker

Edited by Virginia Ann Heyerdahl

Published by
Hobby House Press

Grantsville,
Maryland 21536

12

An early 1934 publicity shot of Shirley Temple
at 20th Century Fox Studios. She is wearing
the costume from *Stand Up and Cheer* and
proudly displays her wigged *Patsy Lou* in
riding jodhpurs.

Additional copies of this book may be purchased at $29.95 (plus postage and handling)
from
Hobby House Press, Inc.
1 Corporate Drive
Grantsville, Maryland 21536
or from your favorite bookstore or dealer.

Table of Contents

Acknowledgments

The author can never emphasize enough the help received from the many collectors who love to share their dolls. Many of the dolls have changed owners since this study was first begun. For everyone who has loaned dolls or sent photographs and information, we are deeply grateful and appreciative.

To my husband, John, I am most indebted for the many photographs he has taken over the years plus all the help he has given to assist in the completion of the book.

To our publisher, Gary Ruddell, for backing this project and our ever-helpful and supportive editor, Virginia Ann Heyerdahl, we could not be more thankful.

The author, Patty Bewley (Schoonmaker), at age 2½ when she resembled a "Patsy" doll herself!

Introduction

In this second volume of in-depth research on Effanbee dolls, we present the result of studies conducted over several decades of our doll collecting years. We will herein cover only part of the gleaned material to be followed by another volume dealing with the beloved *Patsy* family and its variants.

To cover the entire doll family in one volume would have involved sacrificing some of the information to fit into a reasonable space. We have broken down categories for greater clarity and understanding so that special edition dolls have their own coverage. (Many times the wig and original costuming decreed the true identity of the doll, not the marking on the head and/or torso previously used for an earlier model.) Hence, wherever possible, we searched out the original advertising in old catalogs and we studied the trade magazines in the Library of Congress.

As we stated in our Introduction to Volume I, **Effanbee Dolls The Formative Years, 1910-1929**, the Effanbee Corporation lost a large case of printed material dating back many years when moving from Manhattan to Brooklyn in 1958.

Therefore, each piece of advertising in magazines or catalogs or small folios and *The Patsytown News* saved by collectors are doubly treasured and help tell the story of this prestigious manufacturer of composition dolls.

To this, we add the photographic study of the actual dolls themselves, their wardrobes and accessories. This author prefers to present the material, in most instances, in chronological order. Therefore, the chapters are arranged in the order in which the dolls were presented to the public.

Due to contact with composition doll collectors through our column "Compo Corner" in **Doll Reader**® magazine, we are often surprised to learn some *Patsy* collectors are not aware of the existence of the mama doll *Patsy* (later to become *Marilee*). We are pleased to present the earlier version in her many variations.

The *Patsys* which follow are very well-known to the collectors, yet some of the rarer versions may come as a surprise and begin "the thrill of the chase" for that special edition. Happy searching!

The next volume will include details on the *George Washington Bicentennial Dolls, Patsy Mae, Patsy Ruth*, the mysterious *Patsy Alice, Wee Patsy, Patricia*, the rare *Patricia-Kin*, the *Tyrolean* dolls, the movie *Anne Shirley* dolls, *Patsy Babykin, Babyette* and *Patsy Tinyette* plus details from Effanbee's publication *The Patsytown News*.

We hope this book adds to the enrichment of your collecting. With the extensive variety of Effanbee dolls, some of which are rare or in limited supply, very few of us can own each version. Yet, with photographs and the recorded history, each of us can own them all "in knowledge." Enjoy!

Patricia N. Schoonmaker

Chapter One

Patsy/Marilee
Mama Dolls

1

To this day, many collectors are not aware that Effanbee made a cloth-bodied mama doll named *Patsy* before it created the all-composition doll, originally named *Mimi*, whose name was changed within one month to *Patsy*.

Many researchers have struggled to pin down a date for the swing-leg mama doll, some of which were 30in (76cm) tall. Strangely enough, there are no specific advertisements on this beautiful, very high quality doll. The eyes have been inserted by machine into the solid-top bald head (for a wig) without the necessity of cutting and regluing the top of the head, as was done earlier.

The late Louella Hart had listed dates for this doll as 1924 to 1926 and we felt this was probably correct at the time we self-published our book, *The Effanbee Patsy Family and Related Types*, in 1971. However, in the ensuing years, we realized the tool to insert eyes in a solid-top head had not been in use that early, after comparing other dolls known to have been made in this period.

The first marked *Rosemary* was announced to the trade early in 1926. One smaller model, marked "Rosemary," has the cutaway head top (reglued under the wig) but all the others have the solid dome under the wig. Hence, the cloth torso swing-leg *Patsy* would date from 1926 or later.

One doll model, marked "Rosemary," has the same mold arms and legs as our marked cloth-bodied *Patsy* (see *Illustration 386* in **Effanbee Dolls The Formative Years, 1910-1929**). The leg shape has the unique baby creases on the thigh above the knee. Since this doll was completely original and the identical doll was also advertised in the Montgomery Ward catalog for 1927, this is almost certainly the date of the mama doll *Patsy* as well.

Effanbee, in its official statement of facts in applying for a trademark for the name "Patsy," declared it had been using the name on dolls since September 15, 1927.

By 1928, the very same swing-leg mama doll, which was much too appealing to simply discontinue, was renamed *Marilee*. Our own collection has each doll in the 22in (56cm) size. The finely woven, strong muslin *Patsy* body had been redesigned with the front in two shaped sections and a somewhat slimmer waist. The baby leg creases had been smoothed out and the dimples in the knees eliminated. The intent appears to have been to make her into a little older child. Original advertising on the all-composition *Patsy* described her as being only three years old.

The smaller 14½in (37cm) swing-leg *Patsy* mama doll is difficult to locate. Much more prevalent are the small cloth-bodied versions with complete composition legs to the torso. The shoulder heads were done in many forms. There were painted eyes, blue-gray metal sleep eyes and

Illustration 2. Back of the shoulder head of the 22in (56cm) *Patsy* mama doll, seen in *Illustration 1*, showing the marking: "EFFANBEE//PATSY//COPYR.// DOLL."

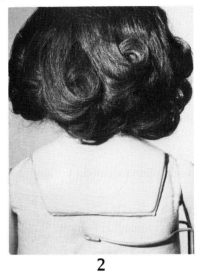

2

Illustration 1. 22in (56cm) *Patsy* mama doll; composition shoulder head, cloth body, slender well-proportioned composition arms with dimples in the elbows, composition legs to above the knees with baby wrinkles on the inside upper legs; brown human hair wig; blue-gray tin sleep eyes, multi-stroke (four) eyebrows, real hair upper eyelashes, painted upper and lower eyelashes, an open mouth with four teeth. This doll has a very high quality of painting of the peaches and cream shades before the suntan shades came into vogue.

4

Illustration 4. 22in (56cm) *Patsy* mama doll, seen in *Illustrations 1, 2* and *3*, shown wearing her original yellow cotton voile dress with white dotted swiss square collar and blue ribbon bow.

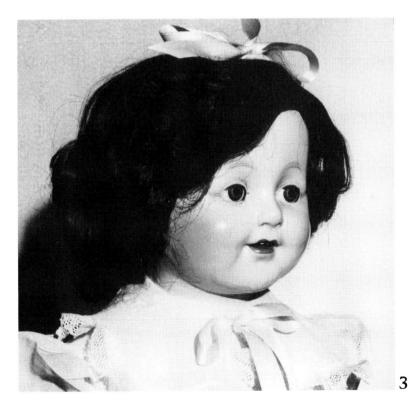

3

Illustration 3. Close-up of the 22in (56cm) *Patsy* mama doll, seen in *Illustrations 1* and *2*, showing the detail of the painting.

glassene eyes. Some of the heads were of heavier composition and there were molded painted hair and wig models, as well as those with closed mouths and open mouths with teeth.

The company did not run advertisements or new articles on the smaller cloth-bodied *Patsy*, but she is shown in a group photograph as late as 1931 and may have been on the market even longer. She made a nice contrast to the sober *Patsy*, with her cheerful smile, when a child (or future adult collector) owned both versions.

Marilee was said to be new for Christmas in 1928. We included two contemporary photographs in among the mama dolls in our first Effanbee book. Yet she is part of the *Patsy* story, so she is shown in this volume as well.

Included in a news story on the new *Skippy* in the February 1929 *Toys and Novelties* magazine is this paragraph: "In the line of mama dolls, Marilee has an extensive new wardrobe with some beautiful dresses, coats and hats."

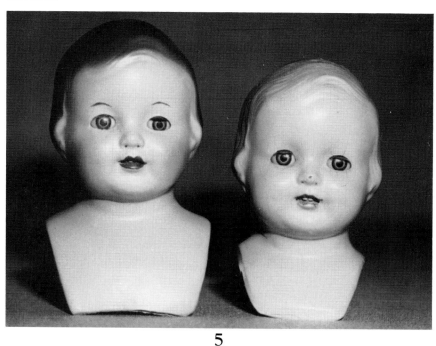

Illustration 5. Shoulder heads to 16in (41cm) and 14in (36cm) *Patsy* dolls; composition; painted hair; blue metal sleep eyes, human hair eyelashes, painted lower eyelashes, open mouths with two teeth each and felt tongues.

5

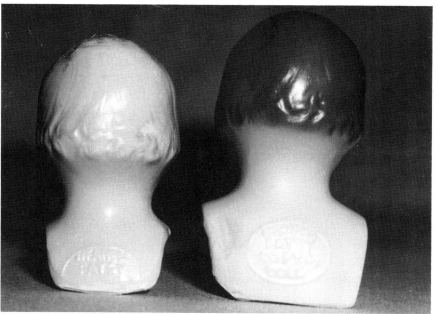

6

Illustration 6. The backs of the shoulder heads to the 14in (36cm) and 16in (41cm) *Patsy* dolls, seen in *Illustration 5*, showing the markings. The 14in (36cm) blonde-haired doll is marked: "EFFANBEE//PATSY" in a half oval; the 16in (41cm) brown-haired doll is marked: "EFFANBEE//PATSY// COPYR.//DOLL" in an oval.

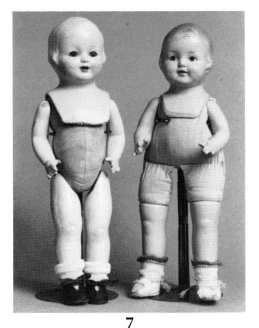

7

8

Illustration 8. 14in (36cm) *Patsy*, seen in *Illustration 7*, in her original multi-colored cotton dress with white collar. *Photograph courtesy of Ethel Stewart.*

Illustration 10. 14½in (37cm) *Patsy* dolls; composition heads, cloth bodies, composition arms and legs. The doll on the left has blonde painted hair, blue painted eyes, single-stroke eyebrows and an open/closed mouth. The doll on the right has a brown wig, gray-blue metal sleep eyes, single-stroke eyebrows and an open mouth with two teeth. The doll on the left is wearing her original red and white cotton dress with a white piqué collar with red braid. A red ribbon bow with streamers is missing at the neck. They are both marked: "EFFANBEE//PATSY" in half circles on the shoulder heads.

Illustration 7. 14½in (37cm) and 14in (36cm) *Patsy* dolls; composition heads, cloth bodies with cry voices, composition arms and legs; blonde molded and painted hair; blue painted eyes, light eyebrows. The 14½in (37cm) *Patsy* on the left has an open mouth with teeth and is marked on the back of the shoulder head: "EFFANBEE//PATSY//COPYR.//DOLL" in an oval. The 14in (36cm) *Patsy* on the right has a closed mouth and is marked on the back of the shoulder head: "EFFANBEE//PATSY" in a half oval. *Photograph courtesy of Ethel Stewart.*

10

9

Illustration 9. 14½in (37cm) swing-leg *Patsy* mama doll; composition shoulder head (trimmed down type), cloth body, composition arms with the two center fingers bent in towards the palms, composition legs with molded knees and cloth tops; brown mohair wig with stitched part; blue metal sleep eyes, single arched eyebrows, real hair upper eyelashes, painted lower eyelashes, an open mouth with teeth and a felt tongue behind the teeth; marked on the back of the shoulder head: "EFFANBEE//PATSY" in a half circle. She is dressed in a pink romper of cotton broadcloth which has blue flowers and maroon bows on it. The romper has a white piqué collar as well as white piqué cuffs and ties on the matching bonnet. The label at the neck back reads: "A Molly-'es PRODUCT//American Made." The garment would have been purchased separately from the doll. *Rosemary Hanline Collection.*

Illustration 11. 14in (36cm) *Patsy*; composition shoulder head, cloth body, composition arms and legs; unpainted molded hair, brown sleep eyes, light tan eyebrows, human hair upper eyelashes, an open mouth with four teeth and a felt tongue; wears her original dotted swiss dress with rose print design and plain ruffles around the bottom and the neck; marked on the back of the shoulder head: "EFFANBEE// PATSY" in a half circle; circa 1932. A doll with this same dress material was included in the F.A.O. Schwarz Christmas catalog for 1932. *Dorothy Tonkin Collection. Photograph by David Carlson.*

Illustration 12. Close-up of the 14in (36cm) *Patsy*, seen in *Illustration 11*, showing the marking. *Dorothy Tonkin Collection. Photograph by David Carlson.*

Illustration 13. 14in (36cm) *Patsy*; composition head, cloth body, composition arms and legs; blonde mohair wig; green glassene sleep eyes, light one-stroke eyebrows, real hair upper eyelashes, painted lower eyelashes, an open mouth with two teeth; marked on the back of the shoulder head: "EFFANBEE//PATSY" in a half circle. *Marge Meisinger Collection.*

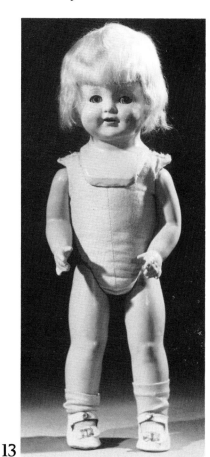

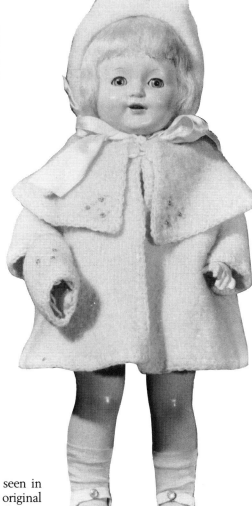

Illustration 14. 14in (36cm) *Patsy*, seen in *Illustration 13*, wearing her possibly original hand-embroidered pink blanket-cloth cap, coat and muff. *Marge Meisinger Collection.*

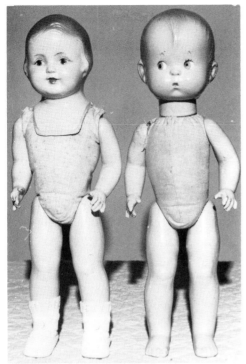

15

Illustration 15. Comparison of a 14in (36cm) *Patsy* and a 14½in (37cm) *Skippy*. Both have composition shoulder heads, cloth bodies, composition arms and legs; blonde painted hair; blue painted eyes, brown eyebrows, painted eyelashes and open/closed mouths.

Illustration 16. Back view of the 14in (36cm) *Patsy* and 14½in (37cm) *Skippy*, seen in *Illustration 15*, showing the markings. *Patsy* is marked on the back of her shoulder head: "EFFANBEE//PATSY" in a half circle; *Skippy* is marked on the back of his neck: "EFFANBEE//SKIPPY//©//P.L. Crosby."

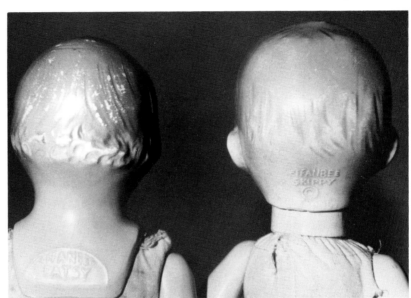

16

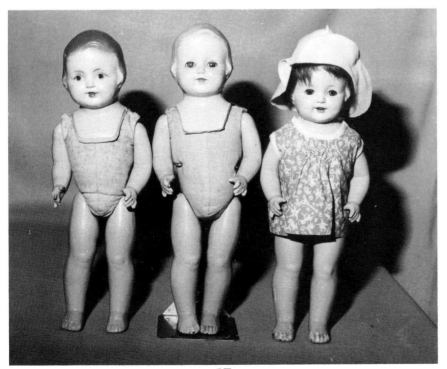

17

Illustration 17. Three versions of the 14in (36cm) *Patsy* doll. The doll on the left has painted eyes and an open/closed mouth. The middle doll has metal eyes with eyelashes and an open/closed mouth. The doll on the right has metal eyes and an open mouth with two teeth.

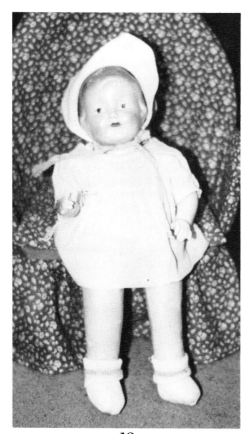

18

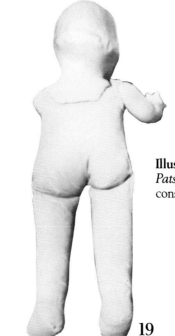

Illustration 19. Back view of the 14in (36cm) *Patsy*, seen in *Illustration 18*, showing the body construction. *Cleone Dixon Collection.*

Illustration 18. 14in (36cm) *Patsy*; composition shoulder head, peach-colored cloth torso and legs, full composition arms which are jointed inside; reddish-blonde painted hair; two-tone blue eyes, painted eyebrows, an open/closed mouth; marked "EFFANBEE//PATSY" in a half oval on the back of the shoulder head. She is wearing her original pale blue organdy dress and bonnet over a combination undergarment. *Cleone Dixon Collection.*

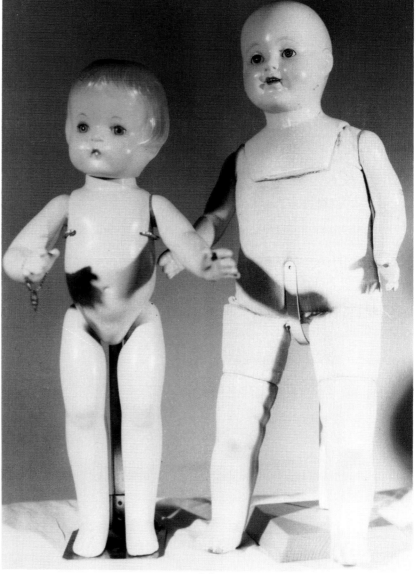

Illustration 20. 19in (48cm) *Patsy Ann* with her ancestor, a 22in (56cm) cloth-bodied *Patsy* mama doll. *Patsy Ann* is all composition. *Patsy* has a composition shoulder head with a solid or bald head on a cloth body with composition arms and legs above the knees. Her eyes were inserted without slicing the top of the head as was the practice with earlier mama dolls.

20

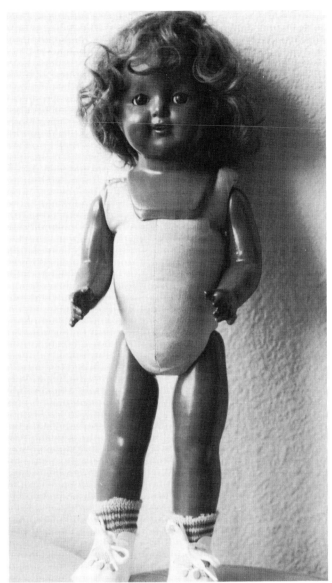

21

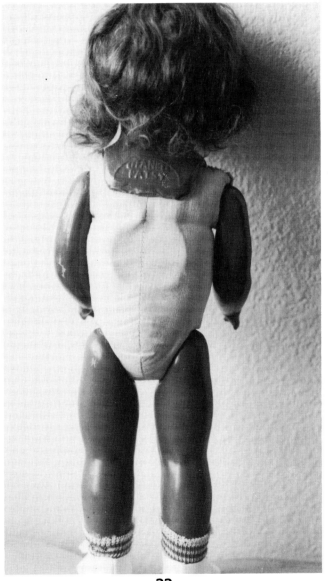

22

Illustration 21. 15in (38cm) black *Patsy*; composition shoulder head, cloth body, composition arms and legs; brown mohair wig; brown metal eyes, brown eyebrows, real hair upper eyelashes, painted lower eyelashes, an open mouth with four teeth and a felt tongue, molded ears; voice box in torso; marked on the back of the shoulder plate, under a half circle: "EFFANBEE//PATSY;" circa late 1920s, early 1930s. Black dolls in this time period were made "to special order" and were not part of the regular line. *Sylvia Lehn Collection. Photograph by Sylvia Lehn.*

Illustration 22. Back view of the 15in (38cm) black *Patsy*, seen in *Illustration 21*, showing the marking and the voice box. *Sylvia Lehn Collection. Photograph by Sylvia Lehn.*

24

23

Illustration 24. Close-up of the marking on the back of the 30in (76cm) *Patsy*, seen in *Illustration 23*. Note the label on the back of the original dress which reads: "EFFANBEE//DOLL//FINEST & BEST" in an oval and underneath "MADE IN U.S.A." *Nancy Carlson Collection. Photograph by David Carlson.*

Illustration 23. 30in (76cm) *Patsy*; composition shoulder head, cloth body, composition arms and legs to above the knees; ash blonde human hair wig in long curls; blue-gray eyes, brown multi-stroke eyebrows, human hair upper eyelashes, painted lower eyelashes, an open mouth with two teeth and a metal tongue, molded ears; marked on the back of the shoulder plate: "EFFANBEE//PATSY//COPYR.//DOLL" in an oval; circa 1927. *Nancy Carlson Collection. Photograph by David Carlson.*

Illustration 25. 30in (76cm) *Patsy*, seen in *Illustration 23*, shown in her original labeled pale green voile dress which has pink and green ribbon trim and lace at the neck, hem and dress front, a one-piece combination undergarment, a separate slip and she is wearing her original hair bow (her shoes are not original). *Nancy Carlson Collection. Photograph by David Carlson.*

25

14

Illustration 27. 30in (76cm) *Patsy Mae, Mae Starr* and, seated, *Patsy,* shown for comparison. *Mae Starr* and *Patsy* are circa 1927. *Mae Starr* and *Patsy, Nancy Carlson Collection; Patsy Mae, Dorothy Tonkin Collection. Photograph by David Carlson.*

26

Illustration 26. 30in (76cm) *Patsy,* seen in *Illustrations 23 and 25,* shown here with a 30in (76cm) *Mae Starr,* on the right, for comparison. *Mae Starr* has a composition shoulder head, a cloth body, composition arms and legs to above the knees; brunette human hair wig; light blue-gray eyes, brown eyebrows, human hair upper eyelashes, painted lower eyelashes, an open mouth with four teeth and a metal tongue, molded ears; wears a combination undergarment with bloomer legs and cuffs of deeper pink, an attached slip designed with a slit so that her mechanism can be worked, a pink dotted swiss dress with white lace trim topped by a rosette edged in burgundy; dress is labeled: "EFFANBEE//DOLL//FINEST & BEST" in an oval and underneath "MADE IN U.S.A.;" circa 1927. *Nancy Carlson Collection. Photograph by David Carlson.*

27

29

Illustration 28. 24in (61cm) *Marilee*; composition shoulder head, cloth body, composition arms and legs up to above the knees; dark brown curly human hair wig; blue-gray glassene eyes, multi-stroke brown eyebrows, real hair upper eyelashes, painted upper and lower eyelashes, an open mouth with two teeth; marked on the back of the shoulder head: "EFFANBEE// MARILEE//DOLL;" circa 1928. *Nancy Carlson Collection. Photograph by David Carlson.*

Illustration 29. The marking on the back of the 24in (61cm) *Marilee*, seen in *Illustration 28*. Note that the marking is not in the usual oval. *Nancy Carlson Collection. Photograph by David Carlson.*

Illustration 30. 30in (76cm) *Marilee*; composition shoulder head, cloth body, composition arms and legs; brown human hair wig; blue tin sleep eyes, painted eyebrows, real hair upper eyelashes, painted upper and lower eyelashes, an open mouth with four teeth; marked: "EFFANBEE// MARILEE//COPR//DOLL" in an oval; circa 1928. She wears a real child's peach-colored smocked dress. *Bothwell/Chapman Collection. Photograph by owner.*

30

28

31

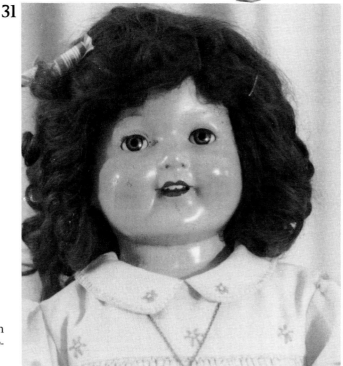

Illustration 31. Close-up of the 30in (76cm) *Marilee*, seen in *Illustration 30*, showing the detail of her face. *Bothwell/Chapman Collection. Photograph by owner.*

Color Illustration 1. 30in (76cm) *Patsy*; composition shoulder head, arms and legs to above the knees; dark blonde human hair wig of long curls; blue tin sleep eyes, real hair upper eyelashes, multi-stroke painted eyebrows, an open smiling mouth with teeth; wears original labeled pink dress with shirred yoke and tiered lace trim on the skirt; head is marked: "EFFANBEE//PATSY//COPR.// DOLL;" 1927. *Nancy Carlson Collection. Photograph by David Carlson.*

LEFT: Color Illustration 2. Close-up of the 30in (76cm) *Patsy,* seen in *Color Illustration 1. Nancy Carlson Collection. Photograph by David Carlson.*

RIGHT: Color Illustration 3. 22in (56cm) *Patsy*; composition shoulder head, arms and legs to above the knees; brown human hair wig; blue tin eyes, real hair upper eyelashes, multi-stroke eyebrows, an open smiling mouth with teeth; wears original labeled yellow voile dress with a white dotted swiss lace-edged collar; head is marked: "EFFANBEE// PATSY//COPR.//DOLL;" 1927.

BELOW: Color Illustration 4. Close-up of the 22in (56cm) *Patsy*, seen in *Color Illustration 3*.

BELOW: Color Illustration 5. 14½in (37cm) *Patsy*; composition head, arms and legs, cloth torso; golden painted hair with molded marks; blue painted two-toned eyes, dark painted eyelashes, an open/closed smiling mouth with dimples in each cheek; wears original red and white checked dress with red stitching at the hem top and a white collar trimmed in red braid; 1927.

RIGHT: Color Illustration 6. 14in (36cm) *Mimi, Patsy's* predecessor. *Nancy Carlson Collection. Photograph by David Carlson.*

BELOW RIGHT: Color Illustration 7. Close-up of the marking on the back of the 14in (36cm) *Mimi,* seen in *Color Illustration 6.* The marking reads: "EFFanBEE//Mi-Mi//PAT.PEND//DOLL." *Nancy Carlson Collection. Photograph by David Carlson.*

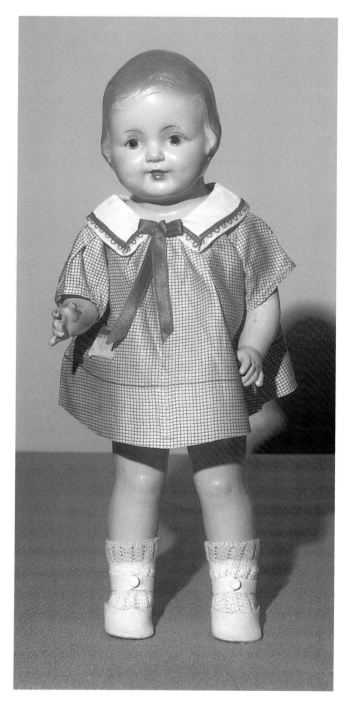

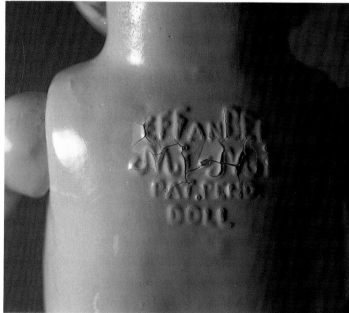

19

RIGHT: Color Illustration 8. All-original sleep-eyed wigged *Patsy* with her original box, wearing a fur coat and hat. *Patsy Moyer Collection. Photograph by Patsy Moyer.*

ABOVE: Color Illustration 9. Close-up of the all-original *Patsy*, seen in *Color Illustration 8. Patsy Moyer Collection. Photograph by Patsy Moyer.*

LEFT: Color Illustration 11. Two *Patsy* dolls and a *Patsy Brother* (in the center) wearing labeled Effanbee cotton costumes.

BELOW: Color Illustration 10. Three *Patsy* dolls, left to right: painted hair *Patsy* in her original yellow silk party dress; red-wigged *Patsy* in her labeled party outfit; painted hair *Patsy* in her green print school dress.

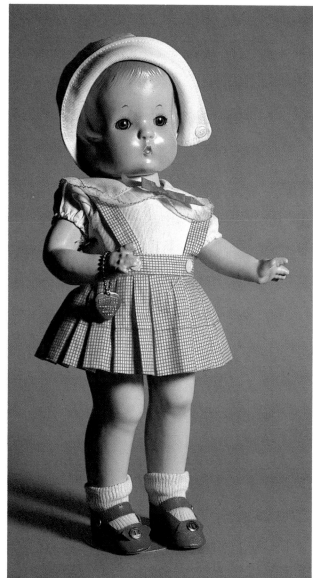

ABOVE: Color Illustration 12. All-original *Patsy* with her gold paper heart-shaped tag. *Florence Mosseri Collection.*

ABOVE RIGHT: Color Illustration 13. All-original sleep-eyed *Patsy*. *Nancy Carlson Collection. Photograph by David Carlson.*

RIGHT: Color Illustration 14. All-original *Patsy Brother* with his original box, wearing a cotton print and felt costume and *Patsy* wearing a felt coat and beret by Effanbee. *Nancy Carlson Collection. Photograph by David Carlson.*

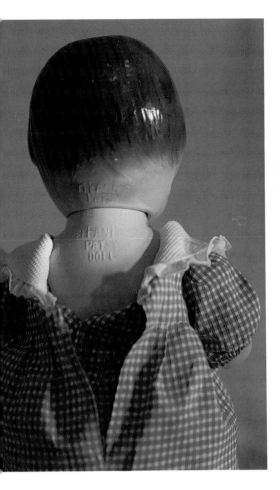

RIGHT: Color Illustration 16. Sleep-eyed
Patsy in a cotton play dress. *Nancy Carlson
Collection. Photograph by David Carlson.*

ABOVE: Color Illustration 17. Close-up of
the marking on the back of the sleep-eyed
Patsy, seen in *Color Illustration 16.*

ABOVE: Color Illustration 19. Two *Patsys*, one wearing a handmade pink party outfit and the other in a woven voile cotton dress by Effanbee.

RIGHT: Color Illustration 18. *Patsy* wearing a yellow silk party frock by Effanbee.

LEFT: Color Illustration 20. 13½in (34cm) rare Chinese *Patsy* in a hand-made brocade outfit. *Dorothy Tonkin Collection.*

ABOVE: Color Illustration 21. Back view of the 13½in (34cm) rare Chinese *Patsy*, seen in *Color Illustration 20. Dorothy Tonkin Collection.*

OPPOSITE PAGE: Color Illustration 22. Close-up of the 13½in (34cm) rare Chinese *Patsy*, seen in *Color Illustrations 20* and *21.*

RIGHT: **Color Illustration 23.** Close-up of a rare Chinese *Patsy* with painted side-glancing eyes. *Gay Lawson Collection. Photograph by Joel S. Lawson, Jr.*

BELOW: **Color Illustration 24.** Close-up of the hand-stitched shoes with embroidery on the toes, from the rare Chinese *Patsy*, seen in *Color Illustration 23. Gay Lawson Collection. Photograph by Joel S. Lawson, Jr.*

ABOVE LEFT: Color Illustration 29. Back view of the rare Indian *Patsy*, seen in *Color Illustration 28*, showing the original label. *The late Sara Barrett Collection.*

LEFT: Color Illustration 27. Rare Chinese *Patsy* in a dark blue brocade, a blue ribbon winner. *Judy Johnson Collection.*

ABOVE: Color Illustration 28. Rare Indian *Patsy* in an original labeled outfit. *The late Sara Barrett Collection.*

ABOVE: Color Illustration 31. *Texas Centennial Patsy* with a cloth body. *Photograph by Polly Judd.*

RIGHT: Color Illustration 32. Close-up of the *Texas Centennial Patsy*, seen in *Color Illustration 31. Photograph by Polly Judd.*

Chapter Two

Mimi/Patsy
and Their Creator

The *Mimi/Patsy* naming of one doll is an intriguing mystery which no doubt would have been perfectly explainable in her own day, before the details were lost. When we were preparing the research in 1970 for our self-published book, *The Effanbee Patsy Family and Related Types*, we applied for a number of trademark registrations from the United States Department of Commerce Patent Office.

The first trademark we requested was for *Mi-mi* (so marked on the doll) but actually advertised as *Mimi*. Effanbee often has discrepancies in the spelling on names of dolls between the original publicity and the actual created version from the factory.

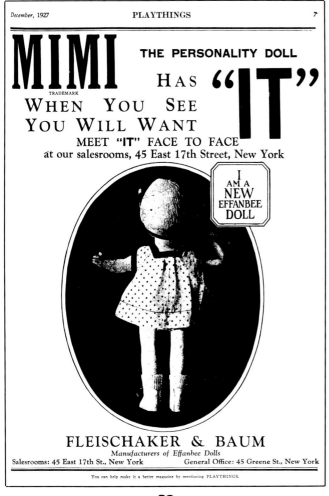

32

33

Illustration 32. Advertisement from the December 1927 *Playthings* trade magazine for *Mimi*, presumably a little French doll.

Illustration 33. Advertisement from the January 1928 *Playthings* trade magazine for *Patsy*, a little Irish doll. Note that the advertisement is the same, except for the name change, as the one shown in *Illustration 32*.

In December 1927, *Playthings* trade magazine advertised: "Mimi, The Personality Doll. Mimi Has 'It,' When You See 'It,' You Will Want 'It,' Meet 'It' Face To Face at our salesrooms, 45 East 17th Street, New York. I am a NEW Effanbee Doll." *Toys and Novelties* ran the same full-page advertisement, with the printing slightly rearranged.

By the very next month, *Playthings* ran the very same advertisement except that the name *Mimi* had been changed to *Patsy*. Upon receiving *Patsy's* trademark papers, we were informed by the Director of the Examining Operation of the Patent Office that the trademark "Mi-Mi," the subject of application serial number 256,079, never matured into a registration, but was abandoned and the file destroyed.

The "Patsy" trademark, number 238,800, was registered on February 14, 1928, on Valentine's Day, most fitting for such a love of a doll. Effanbee stated that it had been using the name since September 15, 1927. This evidently was the debut of the cloth-bodied mama doll *Patsy*, **if** an accurate date was given. The all-composition *Patsy* was first advertised, as such, in January 1928.

A researcher ponders what could have happened in one month's time to change a doll's name and the color of her eyes and hair! *Mimi* had blue eyes but early *Patsys* had an unusual olive-brown eye color. We came upon a small paragraph in a 1928 *Toy World* trade magazine which read:

"Effanbee Dolls
"The large line of dolls manufactured by Fleischaker & Baum was displayed at the [toy] fair by A. P. Shannon, Pacific Coast representative. The place of honor in the beautifully decorated

Illustration 34. Letter from the Patent Office of the United States Department of Commerce explaining that the trademark "Mi-mi" never matured into a registration, but was abandoned and the file destroyed.

U.S. DEPARTMENT OF COMMERCE
Patent Office

Address Only: COMMISSIONER OF PATENTS
Washington, D.C. 20231

September 24, 1970

Dear Mrs. Schoonmaker:

Enclosed are copies of eleven trademark registration, which cost twenty cents each, and a copy of the Read Patent No. 1,283,558 which costs fifty cents, as requested in your letter dated August 4, 1970.

The first item in your letter, the trademark "Mi-mi" subject of application Serial No. 256,079 is not available. That application never matured into a registration, but was abandoned and the file has since been destroyed.

With your letter you enclosed a fee of $3.00. The total cost of these copies is $2.70. The question of refund of thirty cents is being referred to Finance Division.

Very truly yours,

C. M. Wendt
Director, Trademark
Examining Operation

DAUGHTER OF FAMOUS FATHER LIKES DOLLS

Here's six-year-old "Patsy" Fitzmaurice as New York has seen her on three occasions. At the left she's being given a new doll by Dr. Louis Harris, New York Health Commissioner; upper right, as she arrived from Ireland; large photo shows "Patsy" as guest of honor at a Central Park May Fete.

Illustration 35. Article from an unspecified Tacoma, Washington, newspaper of May 9, 1928, about six-year-old "Patsy" Fitzmaurice.

room was accorded to the Patsy dolls, which are at the present the 'talk of the country,' according to 'Pete.' A picture of Patricia Fitzmaurice, daughter of the trans-Atlantic aviator, holding the first Patsy doll, adorned the wall."

Almost surely, this child was responsible for the *Mimi/Patsy* name change. Yet, if she were, some of the Effanbee executives (possibly "Pete" Shannon) must have made her acquaintance prior to her famous father's first east-west Atlantic crossing which took place April 12th to the 13th, 1928.

Patsy was an association doll as well as a sales cycle doll. Effanbee was quick to present dolls which fit into current history, including sailor, soldier and nurse dolls during the World War I era, as well as the *Salvation Army Lass* in 1921.

Aviators, beginning with Charles Lindbergh, would come to be greatly idolized with the development of flight. In 1925, in the United States, a board was appointed by President Calvin Coolidge to establish a national policy for the development of all aspects of aviation.

The Air Commerce Act of 1926 was passed at the board's recommendation. The public interest focused on long-range flights, both cross-country and intercontinental. Ambitious individuals endeavored to plan an ocean-crossing flight. Newspapers, for the publicity value, as well as wealthy private citizens, posted enormous prizes for such flights. The *London Daily Mail* offered £10,000 for a non-stop Atlantic crossing and, in 1919, Raymond Orteig established a $25,000 prize for a non-stop flight between New York and Paris. Later, in 1927, first and second prizes of $25,000 and $10,000 were posted by James Dole for a race from California to Hawaii.

From April 12th to the 13th, 1928, the German Junkers monoplane "Bremen" made the first east-west Atlantic Crossing. It took off from Dublin, Ireland, with a crew consisting of the owner, Guenther von Huenefeld, a German baron, and pilots Herman Koehl of Germany and the father of Patricia, James Fitzmaurice, of Ireland.

The crew lost its bearings after 36 hours and, according to David Nevin, author of *The Pathfinders*, by pure luck spotted a lighthouse through a gap in the clouds and landed on a frozen pond on Greenly Island, off the northern tip of Labrador. They missed New York by more than 1000 miles. However, they **had** reached North America, qualifying for the first east-west air crossing of the Atlantic. A photograph in *The Pathfinders* shows the triumphant crew of three sitting up on the back of an open flower-bedecked car on parade in Munich.

From June 17th to the 18th, 1928, Amelia Earhart flew the Atlantic in the monoplane "Friendship." From October 11th to the 15th, the airship "Graf Zeppelin" flew from Frederichshafen, Germany, to Lakehurst, New Jersey, with 23 passengers.

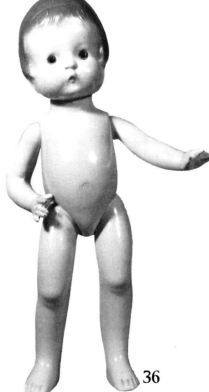

36

Illustration 36. 14in (36cm) *Mimi*, designed by Bernard Lipfert; all composition with two-tone blue eyes; marked on the back of the torso: "EFFanBEE//Mi-Mi//PAT.PEND//DOLL." The original version of the famous *Patsy* doll, *Mimi* was advertised in the December 1927 *Toys and Novelties* and *Playthings* trade magazines. By January 1928, the advertisements read *"Patsy"* not *"Mimi."* *Nancy Carlson Collection. Photograph by David Carlson.*

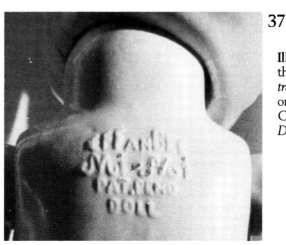

37

Illustration 37. The back of the *Mimi* doll, seen in *Illustration 36*, showing the mark on the torso. *Nancy Carlson Collection. Photograph by David Carlson.*

All of these events would be reflected in the doll and toy world over the years. The McCall pattern company designed pattern number 45, an aviator suit (as well as a knit boy's suit) for *Patsy Brother* dolls. (The only difference between *Patsy* and *Patsy Brother* was in the costuming.) F.A.O. Schwarz of New York sold a *Patsy* doll in an aviator suit.

The author had to go on a big search to discover the identity of Major James Fitzmaurice of the Irish Freestate Airforce, never having been a student of the history of flight. Upon finding the answer, we were all the more desirous of finding a likeness of his little daughter, Patricia, who was shown by Effanbee holding the first *Patsy* doll. Yet it seemed rather hopeless after almost 60 years and we did not know where to begin.

However, a few days later we were leafing through a box of Effanbee related material in our Doll Research Projects files, where we had looked many times before, but now, more aware, noted the name Fitzmaurice. Incredibly enough, here were three photographs of Patsy Fitzmaurice in our own files! They had been sent by a friend because the child was holding a *Patsy* doll. She had a doll in the other arm as well whose head should be showing above the arm of Dr. Louis Harris who is presenting *Patsy*. (Possibly the head of the other doll was airbrushed out of the photograph to focus more attention on the *Patsy* doll.)

The headline and caption of the newspaper article are as follows:

"DAUGHTER OF FAMOUS FATHER LIKES DOLLS.

"Here's six-year-old 'Patsy' Fitzmaurice as New York has seen her on three occasions. At the left she's being given a new doll by Dr. Louis Harris, New York Health Commissioner; upper right, as she arrived from Ireland; large photo shows 'Patsy' as guest of honor at a Central Park May Fete."

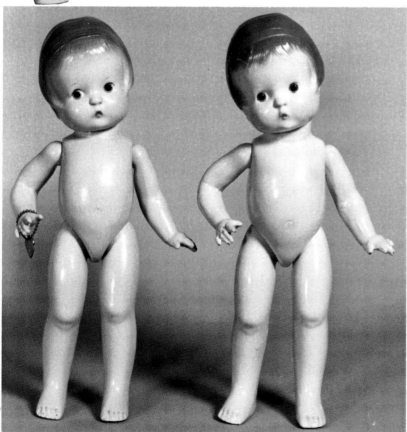

Illustration 38. Comparison of a 14in (36cm) *Patsy* and a 14in (36cm) *Mimi*. *Patsy*, on the left, has brown eyes while *Mimi*, on the right, has blue eyes. *Nancy Carlson Collection. Photograph by David Carlson.*

Illustration 39. 14in (36cm) *Mimi*, shown in *Illustrations 36* and *37*, properly dressed in simple cotton clothes which are not original. *Nancy Carlson Collection. Photograph by David Carlson.*

The news story by Marian Hale reads as follows:

"NEW YORK, May 9 [1928].---'I won't tell you the name of my new doll,' said little Miss Patricia Fitzmaurice, daughter of the famous Bremen flyer, bending over the doll to tie its bonnet.

"That deep dimple on her left cheek twinkled and her bronze-brown eyes shone as she looked up.

"'You've got to guess it,' she said, roguishly.

"Mary Ann? Rosalind? Victoria? Shirley? Cynthia? There were emphatic negatives from her bobbed chestnut head.

"'Give up?' she queried at last. 'You'll never guess it so you might as well.' Defeat admitted, she said:

"'Nancy Hanks. Now guess what color her hair is?'

"'Red? Black? Brown?'

"'It's yellow like gold,' she said, pulling back the bonnet.

"'All of her dresses, besides this one, are my favorite color,' Patsy said. 'Guess what it is?'

"Pink got a nod right away.

"'She's a real American doll 'cause she says Mama,' Patsy informed me. Patsy calls her own mother 'Mommie.'

"Patricia likes American dolls very much. 'Guess how many I have,' she commanded.

"Five? Ten? Fifteen? Twenty?

"'Twenty-two,' she announced. 'But that is counting these ten little ones,' — and she held up a basket of midgets, daintily dressed in pink, blue, yellow organdie. 'But I think we should count them even if they are little 'cause their hats and dresses can come off.'

"She'll Fly Some Day

"Then there came talk about her father, Major Fitzmaurice, of the Irish Freestate Airforce and the Bremen.

"'I have never flown myself,' Patricia remarked. 'She doesn't care to,' her mother put in. 'Why, Mommie, I will so when I grow up to be a big girl,' Patsy insisted.

"Just then a most military figure, Major Walker's personal representative, Major Deegan, came in.

"'Come give me a gallop,' Patsy shouted. When the major was on all fours she jumped on, grabbed his ears for reins, and her merry laugh rang out as they bounced around the room.

"'What do you like best of all to eat?' I asked Patsy when she dismounted. Her usual 'Guess' came quickly.

"Never Ate a Hot Dog

"Strawberries and cream was the first guess. 'Oh, I'm through with them,' she said quickly. Ice cream? Patsy pondered. 'Well, cones,' she said, 'if they're chocolate.'

"'Patricia doesn't care for sweets much,' Mrs. Fitzmaurice helped out. 'She likes substantial dishes.'

"'Oh, Mommie, don't tell,' Patricia admonished her. Hot dogs? She didn't know what they were. Fried chicken? Carrots? Cookies? All received a negative shake of the head. Then inspiration came.

"Irish stew? Instantly the dimple twinkled again and Patricia nodded. 'Especially when it has fresh peas like it did yesterday,' she said.

"One subject she speaks of without making you guess. It is her father.

"'I guess he's about the most wonderfullest man in the world,' she said. 'He says there's nothing to be afraid of anywhere.'

"Likes Her Irish Tea

"At this juncture tea was announced. Patricia laid Nancy Hanks down suddenly. 'Goody.' Then she frowned.

40

Illustration 40. Herr Bernard Lipfert, in 1936, at work in his Brooklyn basement studio sculpting the head of a baby. He was the creator of *Patsy*, his "first love."

"'Bother. It's American tea, isn't it?' She turned to her mother. Then she added a first bit of unsolicited information.

"'I just love tea — Irish tea with milk and sugar. I guess the Irish make the very best tea in the whole world. Don't they, Mommie?'

"Patsy lives at Baldonnel Airdrome just outside Dublin, Ireland. She will be seven on June 21 — 'the longest day in the year,' Patsy volunteered. Her mother is her teacher.

"Fairy tales are her favorite reading. And the Arabian Nights story about the magic carpet that flies."

We learn from the story that Patricia's eyes are bronze-brown and her hair chestnut. Her precocious personality fits publicity descriptions of the *Patsy* doll.

Patsy's "Papa," Herr Bernard Lipfert

A *Newsday* feature story published on March 12, 1974, chronicling the death of Bernard Lipfert, was titled "The Most Marvelous doll in the World" with a subtitle "They were all dolls to Lipfert, but Patsy was his first love. Dolls were his passion. They were born in his basement out of plaster of Paris and clay. Their rosebud mouths and wide-set eyes kept Bernard Lipfert sculpting for nearly 20 years."

The *Newsday* story states that a person 50 years of age [in 1974] might remember *Patsy*, the sad-eyed nymphet of the 1930s who gave rise to the *Patsy* family and made the Effanbee Doll Company, which manufactured *Patsy*, a fortune. She is also said to have made Lipfert an industry star.

Mr. Lipfert's only son, Max, stated in the *Newsday* article that *Patsy* was his father's first love and that Herr Lipfert believed a doll was to be cuddled, not mechanized. He did not believe in gimmickry but went along with the trend of the 1950s and 1960s for battery-operated dolls.

What was there about the *Patsy* doll that elicited such love and devotion in little doll mothers? She was originally planned to sound French (*Mimi*), that is, chic and stylish. This association was dropped in favor of sounding Irish (*Patsy*), to associate with Patricia Fitzmaurice, the daughter of a famous Irish flier.

In actuality, she typified a real little American girl. Children identify with the familiar and her clothes were usually simple copies of what they themselves wore.

The first edition did not cry or even sleep and required a great deal of the child's own imagination to be in use at play. She was absolutely non-intimidating. Later, it was fun to acquire a second version which did sleep and/or which had real hair.

Effanbee merchandising was the most constant of any company. Mr. Hugo Baum, a master at showmanship, was known as the "Ziegfield" of the doll industry. It was a period of great joy for the children whose parents could afford the dolls and of strong yearnings for those who could not. Many people would eventually "collect" them in adulthood.

Effanbee began the industry's second big sales cycle with the beloved *Patsy* doll. (America's first big sales cycle was the *Bye-Lo Baby* doll by Grace Storey Putnam.) Most doll makers are said to have trudged over to see Herr Lipfert at work and negotiated to have him create something similar to attempt to compete with *Patsy*.

However, *Patsy* soon became a family of dolls, and with them was created a new facet of the business — their wardrobes — since, with some few exceptions, dolls prior to this came only with the clothes they wore. A mother or grandmother would make any extra clothing but home sewing would cease to be as prevalent in the late 1920s. The extra commercially made clothing began a new branch of the doll business. This, in turn, opened the way for doll trunks and all manner of accessories and furniture.

Thanks to a first person interview by writer Joan Amundsen, writing in 1974, we gain additional insight into the creation of *Patsy*. Herr Lipfert was extremely talented at designing baby dolls which were greatly in demand but he dreamed of doing something different. According to Amundsen, the artist, on his own decision, designed the *Patsy* doll. He is said to have considered her his biggest and best creation. She apparently did not sell to a manufacturer immediately as she was not a baby and could not say "mama."

However, the Effanbee people were very open to new ideas, and decided to take a chance. This author remembers a former doll club member (who had a doll shop in the *Patsy* era) recalling chats with an Effanbee salesman who stated that the company never expected the doll to be so popular. It was thought that the body was too short and the legs were too long, but "Papa" Lipfert's own creation would be loved by little girls their entire lifetimes.

Joan Amundsen reported on visiting the Lipferts at home where they had moved in the early 1940s to Westbury, Long Island. The studio was set up in the large sun porch on the second floor. The artist retired in about 1964 due to arthritis but had kept this studio just as it was. Joan was allowed to explore the artist's attic which she termed a doll collector's paradise. The most striking object she saw was a life-size model head of the *Patsy* doll with soulful puppy eyes and a rosebud mouth. She wrote, "A doll collector would give five years of childhood for just one walk through that toyland paradise."

An outstanding bit of source data for the doll collecting world was an article in the December 1936 *Fortune* magazine. The article "Dolls — Made in America" described Herr Lipfert's original Brooklyn basement where he might be paid $50 to $500 per original model. The artist was alluded to as "an industry monopoly" with his doll designs which would be made of resin, wood, flour, starch and water. Retail prices ranged from $.25 to $40.

In Brooklyn, he had designed four out of five dolls on the market, being the number one designer of dolls for 25 years. He is quoted in *Fortune* magazine as saying, "Effry doll zat you see in zee stores iss born right there in zis little basement, without any mother, chost a fadder." Herr Lipfert was credited with bringing lifelike expressions into dolls such as the round cheeks, the upturned noses and the rosebud mouths which were considered ideal. The artist believed the toy must not be too realistic but must keep a certain doll-like quality. He had learned his craft in Thüringia, Germany, being a fifth-generation toy maker, coming to the United States in 1912. After many productive decades, he passed away on January 6, 1974, at the age of 87. His creation and "first love," *Patsy*, lives on after him, treasured and appreciated by countless collectors.

Chapter Three

Patsy,

"The Lovable Imp"

Illustration 41. Full-page advertisement for *Patsy*, "The Personality Doll," from the March 1928 issue of *Toy World* magazine. The prototype doll was so new the hair was not yet painted. The shoes were hand-stitched in back and had bow ties. Effanbee had previously used this device of turning a doll's back to the camera to entice buyers into seeking out its salesrooms. Later, Louis Amberg & Son would issue a *Patsy* type which they named *It*.

We now know *Patsy* was once an idea which glimmered in the mind and heart of Herr Bernard Lipfert. She sprang into reality at the touch of his talented hands and Effanbee manufacturers purchased this then "different" doll. She would be first named *Mimi* in late 1927 and advertised as such in January 1928.

Her trademark was issued on Valentine's Day, number 238,800. By January 1929, her makers announced to the trade they had acquired patent number 1,238,558, pertaining to the head and neck joint. This was an effort to deter other manufacturers from issuing look-alikes or something somewhat similar to *Patsy*.

By June of 1928, a full-page advertisement in *Toy World* and other trade publications headlined: "WARNING, if you are a manufacturer, please do not copy PATSY, and if you are a buyer, please do not purchase imitations of

41

42

Illustration 42. Full-page advertisement for *Patsy*, "The Personality Doll," in the October 1928 issue of *Playthings* magazine. There were as yet no gold metal heart-shaped bracelet tags, only the gold paper heart-shaped tags.

PATSY. We request this because we have been informed that the Outstanding Doll Hit of the year has been imitated. Our rights on PATSY cover not only the trademark name, but also the features, characteristics and general appearance. We take this opportunity of courteously requesting respect for our property. Failing in this course our attorneys will take immediate action."

The tide would not be stemmed. Never had a simple little girl doll inspired so many look-alikes. However, that is a story in itself.

The Butler Brothers 1928 catalog included *Patsy* with other Effanbee dolls. She is called "The Hit of the Year" and "A Lovable Imp." *Patsy* is said to have taken the country by storm and would be one of the outstanding successes for this season and many following. Attention was called to the fact that she could stand alone (most earlier cloth stuffed-bodied dolls did not have this ability) and she could be placed in many poses. The heart-shaped trademark paper tag is especially mentioned.

She was listed as being 13½in (34cm) tall, of composition with painted hair, eyes and features and with a tiltable head (many earlier dolls had solid shoulder heads) and movable limbs. Her first clothing was said to be an organdy short dress with lace trim at the neck and sleeves and a full-length lace-trimmed undergarment (a combination suit), cotton socks, slippers and she wore a ribbon bandeau on her head.

An arrival notice in the March 1929 newspaper from the Frederick & Nelson department store in Seattle, Washington, mentioned how loved the adorably real jointed *Patsy* would be. Her new spring wardrobe was also noted.

The first retail catalog appearance appears to be in the Montgomery Ward catalog for 1929. It appears that Effanbee possibly actually introduced two versions of a jointed all-composition girl doll. The same Effanbee artwork — line drawings of the little girl in a combination

Illustration 44. Effanbee, in its statement to the United States Patent Office, claimed that the trademark "Patsy" has been continuously used and applied to said goods in applicants' business since September 15, 1927. This, no doubt, referred to the cloth-bodied mama doll, not the all-composition *Patsy* doll.

Registered Feb. 14, 1928.   Trade-Mark 238,800
UNITED STATES PATENT OFFICE.

FLEISCHAKER & BAUM, OF NEW YORK, N. Y.

ACT OF FEBRUARY 20, 1905.

Application filed October 14, 1927. Serial No. 256,080.

PATSY

STATEMENT.

To the Commissioner of Patents:

Fleischaker & Baum, a firm domiciled in New York city, doing business at No. 45 Greene Street, New York city, N. Y., and composed of the following members, Bernard E. Fleischaker and Hugo Baum, both citizens of the United States, have adopted and used the trade-mark shown in the accompanying drawing, for DOLLS, in Class 22, Games, toys, and sporting goods, and present herewith five specimens showing the trade-mark as actually used by applicants upon the goods, and request that the same be registered in the United States Patent Office in accordance with the act of February 20, 1905, as amended.

The trademark has been continuously used and applied to said goods in applicants' business since September 15th, 1927.

The trademark is applied or affixed to the goods, by placing thereon a printed label or tag on which the trademark is shown.

Applicant hereby appoints Maurice Block, of No. 233 Broadway, borough of Manhattan, city, county, and State of New York (Reg. No. 2289) and his duly authorized agent, their attorney, with full power of substitution and revocation, to prosecute this application, to make alterations and amendments therein, to sign their name to the drawing, to transact all business in the Patent Office connected therewith, and to receive the certificate of registration when issued.

Dated New York, September 27th, 1927.
            FLEISCHAKER & BAUM.
            By HUGO BAUM,
            A Member of the Firm.

43

Illustration 43. Advertisement in the January 1929 issue of *Toy World* magazine in which Effanbee announced in bold headlines that it had acquired the Patent Number 1,283,558 to cover the novel neck and head joint on *Patsy* and other new dolls. This was a bold attempt (but to little effect) to keep other manufacturers from making their look-alike *Patsy* dolls and *Patsy* types.

Patent Number 1,283,558

We are pleased to announce that we have acquired patents that cover the novel neck and head joint on PATSY and our other new dolls.

FLEISCHAKER & BAUM

Salesrooms
45 E. 17th Street

General Office
45 Greene Street

New York, N. Y.

Please mention TOY WORLD when writing to advertisers

44

undergarment or a dress — is used all around both *Patsy* and *Boots* who was said to be like a real American doll.

Effanbee often featured advertisements of two dolls framed in a box, one for the higher priced quality market and one for the so-called "popular priced" market. *Boots'* socket head was the type which fit down into the torso, unlike *Patsy's* head which fit onto a raised neck curve of the torso. *Boots* would not be as finely sanded nor would she have been painted with as many coats. Effanbee may have eventually furnished these for other makers.

Many inner workings of doll production are never made known to the general public, which is understandable, but researchers are becoming aware that manufacturers made certain dolls for themselves and sometimes the same doll for others to dress and wig and christen with a different name entirely.

Boots had the same arms and legs as *Patsy* but an open/closed mouth and a different hairline. She almost surely came from the fertile brain of Herr Lipfert as this was an entirely new creation at this time. (No such records exist but it is possible that Effanbee purchased both designs for purposes of control.)

In 1928, Effanbee sued the Maxine Doll Company of New York City to obtain an injunction against Maxine for making a doll similar to *Patsy* which was marked: "Mitzi//By Maxine//Pat. Pend." We do not have access to the court proceedings, but eventually the appellate court granted Effanbee the exclusive right to a doll having the features, characteristics and general appearance of its design for *Patsy*. (*Mitzi*, who was not too different from the original *Mimi*, also had a sound alike name — Mit-see/Pat-see — as would many others who followed.)

Illustration 46. Advertisement from the Butler Brothers wholesale catalog for 1928 which calls *Patsy* "The Hit of the Year!" and "A Lovable Imp." The ad claimed that *Patsy* had taken the country by storm and indicated she had a heart-shaped trademarked tag (this would be the gold paper heart-shaped tag as the gold metal heart-shaped bracelet tag would not be designed until 1932). A dozen dolls cost $24, wholesale.

Illustration 45. The actual patent, number 1,283,558, which Effanbee claimed protected *Patsy's* neck and head joint. The Colemans, in *The Collector's Encyclopedia of Dolls, Volume Two*, state that in checking on this patent they found it had been obtained about five years earlier (before 1929) and did not actually pertain to the *Patsy* neck joint. Yet Effanbee must have felt this would deter their imitators somewhat.

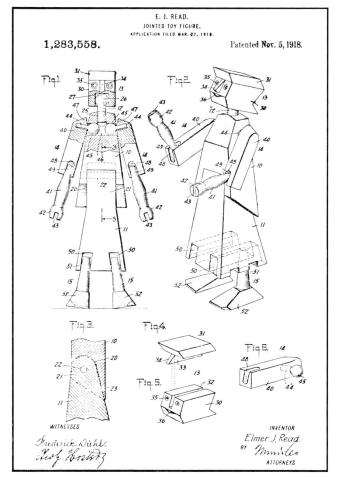

E. J. READ.
JOINTED TOY FIGURE.
APPLICATION FILED MAR. 27, 1918.

1,283,558.

Patented Nov. 5, 1918.

Fig.1. Fig.2. Fig.3. Fig.4. Fig.5. Fig.6.

WITNESSES
Frederick Diehl.

INVENTOR
Elmer J. Read
BY
ATTORNEYS

45

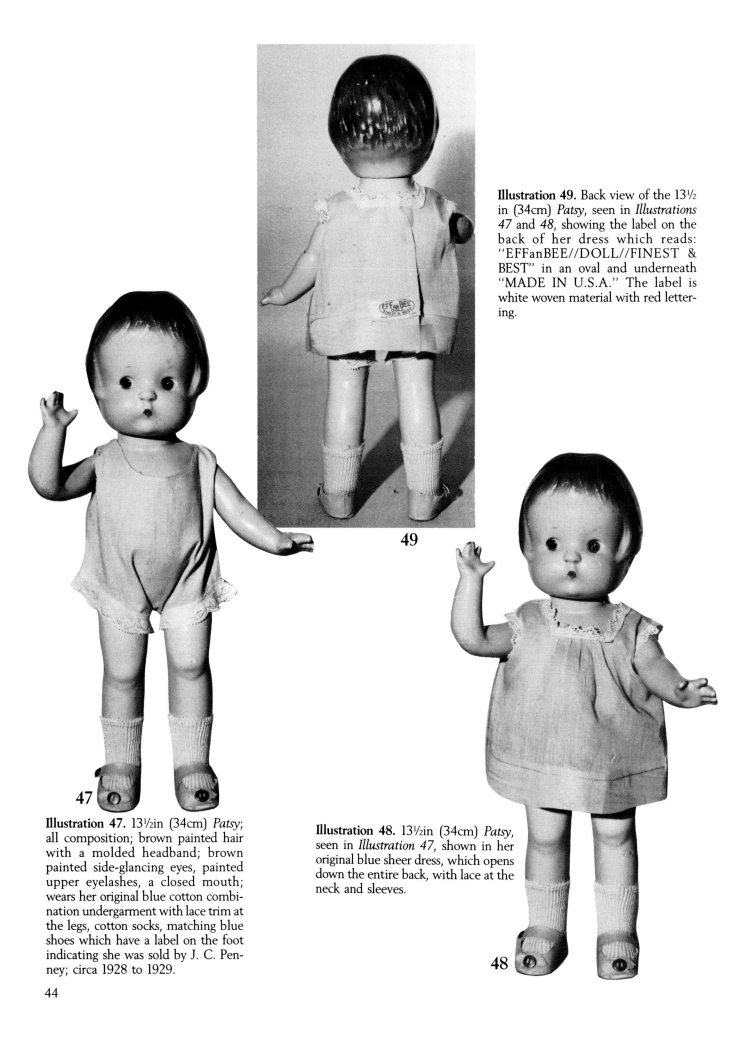

Illustration 49. Back view of the 13½ in (34cm) *Patsy*, seen in *Illustrations 47* and *48*, showing the label on the back of her dress which reads: "EFFanBEE//DOLL//FINEST & BEST" in an oval and underneath "MADE IN U.S.A." The label is white woven material with red lettering.

49

47

Illustration 47. 13½in (34cm) *Patsy*; all composition; brown painted hair with a molded headband; brown painted side-glancing eyes, painted upper eyelashes, a closed mouth; wears her original blue cotton combination undergarment with lace trim at the legs, cotton socks, matching blue shoes which have a label on the foot indicating she was sold by J. C. Penney; circa 1928 to 1929.

Illustration 48. 13½in (34cm) *Patsy*, seen in *Illustration 47*, shown in her original blue sheer dress, which opens down the entire back, with lace at the neck and sleeves.

48

At this distance in time, we collectors find all these dolls very appealing. A collection of *Patsys*, which also included many of the look-alikes, would make a very important historical statement.

The same artwork (line drawings of the *Patsy* doll in her combination undergarment or dress) used with *Patsy* and *Boots*, is repeated in the 1930 advertisement for *Patsy* in the Montgomery Ward catalog. Evidently Effanbee had begun to realize they would never be able to stop all the look-alikes. They now advertise: "American childhood is personified in this dainty Doll. Nationally advertised 'Patsy' is the most widely imitated doll." The copying has now become a fact about which to boast. The advertisement goes on to state: "But the roguish expression, the famous patented tilting head, the unconscious baby grace of arms and legs are the work of an artist and cannot be duplicated. Made entirely of finest American composition — the exquisite child body is so easy to dress. Patsy is adorable in swimming trunks or the laciest party dress." The costume shown in the catalog was a red-checked print with touches of embroidery on the collar and a ribbon bow with long streamers. A scarlet satin hair ribbon, red and white rayon socks and red shoes completed her ensemble. Her price, which was usually set a bit lower in catalogs, was $2.65 rather than the usual $2.95. Some simple little composition dolls at that time were available for as little as $.25, so one *Patsy* doll equaled nearly 12 of the most modestly priced dolls.

The Montgomery Ward catalog in 1930 carried the only Effanbee advertisement located so far for that company's own extra garments. A combination suit, which could serve as a sunsuit, came with a dress of voile sprigged with blue flowers which had a plain bodice and a full skirt and was available for $.89, nearly the cost of four inexpensive dolls.

A special edition of *Patsy* was issued for the 1936 Texas Centennial. For some unknown reason, the all-composition torso has been changed to cloth with an unmarked composition shoulder plate. The separate turning head is marked "EFFANBEE//PATSY," leaving no doubt she is authentic. Her companion is *Skippy*, who wears a cowboy costume to match *Patsy's* cowgirl ensemble. The hats each bear a circular paper label which reads: "Texas Centennial//1936." Other Effanbee models inspired by this event were *Patsy Baby Tinyettes* and *Patsyettes*.

In 1946, Effanbee decided to reissue *Patsy*. The officially photographed prototype doll is shown by Effanbee with the exact same arms as were on the original. By the time she actually came on the retail market, however, the arms were redesigned with rather mitten-like hands. These dolls did not have all the undercoats of paint the original had and many of them, within a few years, were found with all-over surface crazing. However, a few have survived in tiptop shape. *Patsy Joan*, reissued at the same time, had a completely redesigned head yet still bore the Effanbee "family" look. The 1946 *Patsy* now had blue eyes and was not marked in any way which often misleads collectors into believing she is not a genuine Effanbee. She was available in 1947, 1948 and 1949. The reissued *Patsy Joan* is marked "EFFANDBEE" on her torso, with the "D" inserted. A few of the *Little Ladies* are marked this way as well.

The original checked sundress for the 1940s *Patsy* came in blue and white or pink and white with matching embroidery on the pinafore ruffles. Usually the shoes are tie-on slippers except for the roller skates which have gripper snaps.

A very few *Patsy* dolls were made with sleep eyes rather than painted ones, but they are in the 1940s model. Following World War II, metal for eyes may still have been in limited supply. A number of black dolls were made as well. These reissued dolls — white and black — were the final models of Effanbee *Patsy* dolls in composition form.

Illustration 50. 13½in (34cm) *Patsy*; all composition; reddish-brown painted hair with a molded headband; brown painted side-glancing eyes, painted upper eyelashes, a closed mouth; wears a white dimity bloomer dress with blue flowers and an embroidered collar, matching undergarments, replaced shoes; wears a gold paper heart-shaped tag which reads: "EFFANBEE//PATSY//PAT.PEND.// DOLL." *Bothwell/Chapman Collection. Photograph by Noreen Bothwell.*

15. **Original Patsy doll,** winsome expression, movable head and joints, 13 inches, $1.69.

51

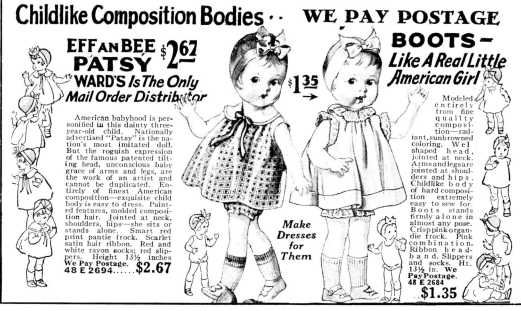

Illustration 52. The first retail advertisement for *Patsy* appeared in the 1929 Montgomery Ward catalog in the St. Paul, Minnesota, edition. The advertisement was for *Boots* as well. The artwork around the edges suggests that both dolls were issued by Effanbee at this time. (This same type of artwork is used in the Effanbee advertisement in the Butler Brothers wholesale catalog and in the 1930 Montgomery Ward catalog.) *Patsy* is described as a "dainty three-year-old child" and the nation's most imitated doll. She is shown wearing a red and white print panty dress (or bloomer dress) made purposely short in order to show her matching panties, red and white rayon socks, red slippers and she has a scarlet satin hair ribbon in her hair. *Boots*, which cost only half as much as *Patsy*, would not be as finely sanded or given as many coats of paint. *Boots* would later be known by other names.

EFFanBEE PATSY

$2.65

American childhood is personified in this dainty Doll. Nationally advertised "Patsy" is the most widely imitated doll.

But the roguish expression, the famous patented tilting head, the unconscious baby grace of arms and legs are the work of an artist and cannot be duplicated.

Made entirely of finest American composition—the exquisite child body is so easy to dress. Patsy is adorable in swimming trunks or the laciest party dress.

Patsy Is Sold by Mail Only by Ward's

Painted features, molded composition hair. Jointed at neck, shoulders, hips—she sits or stands alone in many positions. Smart red print frock with lace edged panties. Scarlet satin hair ribbon. Red and white rayon socks; red slippers. Height 13½ inches. We Pay Postage. 48 G 2694 . . . . **$2.65**

54

Illustration 54. Advertisement in the 1930 Montgomery Ward catalog, the Chicago edition, for a 13½in (34cm) *Patsy*, described as "American childhood...personified in this dainty Doll." The advertisement went on to say that she was said to be the most widely imitated doll. Emphasis was put on the ease of sewing for *Patsy*. Again, the dress color chosen is red and the collar has been embroidered. Her socks are now rayon instead of cotton which the first version wore.

DRESS FOR PATSY

89¢

Designed by Maker of All EFFanBEE Patsy Clothes

Fine soft voile sprigged with tiny blue flowers. The perky binding is of crisp organdie. Real ocean pearl buttons and hand made button holes. Matching pantie-combination (sun suit) has elastic at knees. Finished most daintily and guaranteed to fit Patsy shown above. We Pay Postage. 48 G 953 . . . . **89¢**

55

Illustration 55. The only advertisement ever found for a separate garment made by Effanbee for *Patsy* was in the same 1930 Montgomery Ward catalog, mentioned in *Illustration 54*. Instead of the original straight skirt style, the dress shown is of voile sprigged with tiny blue flowers and it has a full gathered skirt. The neck, armholes and skirt bottom are trimmed in crisp organdy. Real pearl buttons with, surprisingly, handmade buttonholes finished the garment. The matching combination undergarment could double as a sunsuit.

Illustration 56. Dolls sketched in an advertisement from an unnamed Seattle, Washington, newspaper for December 2, 1930. Boy dolls (usually a mate to a girl doll) were in vogue at this time. Rompers were very stylish on boy or girl dolls. Mentioned, but not sketched, are *Baby Dimples* by Horsman and *Patsy* and *Patsykins* — "that inimitable pair...soldier dolls, sailor dolls or Red Riding Hood in miniature." The third doll in the sketch is a *Patsy Brother*. Note the metal heart-shaped bracelet tag drawn on his wrist. The prices for the dolls were $1.25 to $8.95.

Dolls! Dolls! Dolls!

To Delight A Little Girl's Heart

—Wee little dolls for little mothers . . . life-size baby dolls for more competent mothers. Baby Dimples . . . Patsy and Patsykins—that inimitable pair . . . soldier dolls, sailor dolls or Red Riding Hood in miniature. 1.25 to 8.95.

56

57

Illustration 57. Close-up showing the marking on the torso of the first *Patsy* doll: "EFFanBEE//PATSY//PAT.PEND.//DOLL." There were no markings on the head. *Nancy Carlson Collection. Photograph by David Carlson.*

47

Illustration 60. 13½in (34cm) *Patsy;* all composition; wears a red and white cotton dress with a white pique collar embroidered in red, red hair bow; original gold paper heart-shaped tag reads: "This is//TRADE PATSY MARK//PAT. PEND// The Lovable Imp//with tiltable head//and movable limb// AN//EFFanBEE//DOLL." She was advertised in *Good House-keeping* magazine in December 1929. *Florence Mosseri Collection.*

60

59

58

Illustration 59. 13½in (34cm) *Patsy;* all composition; reddish-brown painted hair with a molded headband; painted side-glancing eyes, painted upper eyelashes, a closed mouth; wears her original commercial outfit and a ribbon over the molded headband; marked: "EFFANBEE//PATSY//PAT.PEND.// DOLL;" 1929. The velvet dog has a tag which says: "Bully. Steiff — Original." *Newark Museum Collection (Acc. No. 29.114 a B), Newark, New Jersey.*

Illustration 58. The gold paper heart-shaped tag which came with the *Patsy* dolls. The tag was fastened to the doll's wrist. The doll first issued was marked on the torso and then later on the head and torso. There were no metal heart-shaped bracelet tags until 1932. The tag reads: "This is//TRADE PATSY MARK//PAT. PEND//The Lovable Imp//with tiltable head// and movable limb//AN//EFFanBEE//DOLL."

Illustration 64. Close-up of a 13½in (34cm) *Patsy Brother;* all composition; reddish-brown painted hair with a molded headband; extra large brown painted side-glancing eyes, brown eyebrows, painted upper eyelashes, a closed mouth. *Nancy Carlson Collection. Photograph by David Carlson.*

64

63

Illustration 62. Side view of the 13½in (34cm) *Patsy Brother,* seen in *Illustration 61,* showing the detail of the felt cap. Note his original box. *Inge Simms Collection.*

62

61

Illustration 63. Close-up of the 13½in (34cm) *Patsy Brother,* seen in *Illustrations 61* and *62,* showing the label on the back of the clothing which reads: "EFFanBEE//DOLL//FINEST & BEST" in an oval and underneath "MADE IN U.S.A." *Inge Simms Collection.*

Illustration 61. 13½in (34cm) *Patsy Brother;* all composition; painted hair; brown painted side-glancing eyes, brown eyebrows, painted upper eyelashes, a closed mouth; wears blue felt trousers and a multicolored cotton top all stitched together and a felt cap; marked: "EFFANBEE//PATSY// PAT.PEND.//DOLL." He originally came with a gold paper heart-shaped tag. The metal heart-shaped bracelet tag he is wearing has been added at a later date. This outfit also came on *Patsy Joan Brother.* The only difference in the *Brother* dolls is the clothing. *Inge Simms Collection.*

Illustration 66. 14in (36cm) *Patsy*; all composition; brown painted hair; brown painted side-glancing eyes, brown eyebrows, painted upper eyelashes, a closed mouth; wears an "extra" dress of corded dimity with a deep hem and red and blue flowers, a shawl collar of white batiste with a hemstitched ruffle and a red ribbon bow trim, replaced shoes; marked: "EFFanBEE//PATSY//PAT.PEND.//DOLL;" 1928 to 1929. The dress is a commercial garment. *Nancy Carlson Collection. Photograph by David Carlson.*

66

65

Illustration 65. 14in (36cm) *Patsy*; all composition; brown painted hair; painted side-glancing eyes, a closed mouth; wears a red felt coat with machine-embroidered pockets of green, red and yellow roosters and brass buttons and a matching beret, replaced but old appropriate shoes; marked: "EFFANBEE//PATSY//PAT.PEND.//DOLL;" 1928. *Nancy Carlson Collection. Photograph by David Carlson.*

Illustration 67. 13½in (34cm) *Patsy*; all composition; brown painted hair; brown painted side-glancing eyes, brown painted eyebrows, painted upper eyelashes, a closed mouth; wears a bright red cotton dress with a ruffle at the neck and simulated smocking at the waist in white and blue, white binding and red rickrack on the sleeves, original shoes; 1930s.

67

68

Illustration 68. 13½in (34cm) *Patsy* and *Patsy Brother*; all composition; brown painted hair; brown painted side-glancing eyes, brown painted eyebrows, painted upper eyelashes, closed mouths. Both wear red felt coats with navy blue buttons and two rows of blue stitching trim to create a raglan sleeve look plus stitched sleeve edges and coat bottoms. The girl is wearing a beret while the boy wears a cap with stitched ear flaps.

Illustration 71. 13½in (34cm) *Patsy*; all composition; reddish-brown painted hair; brown painted side-glancing eyes, brown painted eyebrows, painted upper eyelashes, a closed mouth; wears a yellow batiste dress with a white lace-trimmed neckline and armholes and a 1½in (4cm) deep hem with a silk decorative stitch at the hem top, all original combination underwear with lace at the legs; the label is sewn into the hem of the dress on the left back side; 1929 to 1930.

69

Illustration 69. 13½in (34cm) *Patsy* from J. C. Penney, modeling a specialty shop pink silk gown with a square neck bound in blue and two rows of smocking at the neck with ribbon streamers on the shoulders. There is embroidery at the top of the hem. She is marked: "EFFanBEE//PATSY//PAT.PEND.//DOLL." She has no labels and is circa 1928.

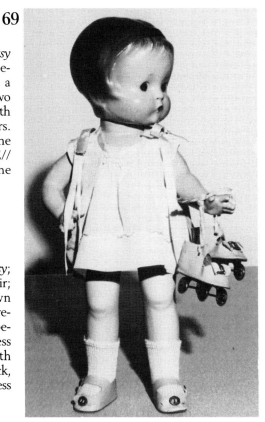

Illustration 70. 13½in (34cm) *Patsy*; all composition; brown painted hair; painted side-glancing eyes, brown painted eyebrows; painted upper eyelashes, a closed mouth; wears a specialty shop blue cotton print dress which opens down the back with white binding at the sleeves and neck, black embroidery effect on the dress front and the top of the hem.

70

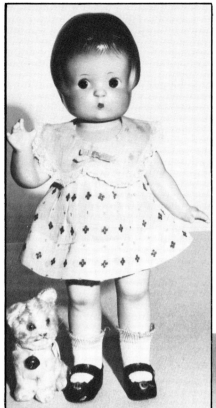

72

Illustration 72. 13½in (34cm) all-original *Patsy*; all composition; wears a voile dress with a woven pattern of red flowers with gold centers between the rows, a pink voile collar edged in lace with a pink silk bow at the neckline, pink bound sleeves on a white background; 1931. This doll was offered as a premium for three *Junior Home* magazine subscriptions in November of 1931.

Illustration 73. 13½in (34cm) *Patsy*; all composition; brown painted hair; painted side-glancing (to the left) eyes, painted upper eyelashes, a closed mouth; wears a print dress with yellow, orange, blue and green circles on a white background with lace at the neck under the bias binding, a matching lace-trimmed combination suit underneath, replaced shoes; circa 1920s.

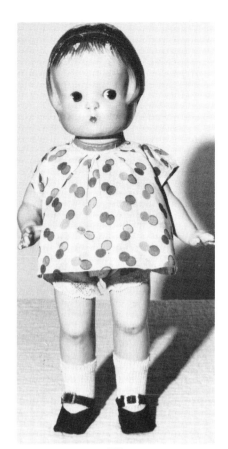

73

74

FANCY DRESS TROUSSEAUX

No. A-2/60/6—Think of the parties you can have for the 13½" **Patsy** doll with all these lovely fancy dress costumes.

Russian costume—White cotton dress bordered with colored print, red velveteen coatee edged with white plush, a cossack hat of white plush and black patent leatherette boots.

Egyptian costume—Gathered, ankle length trousers of blue sateen, with blue, red and gold metallic cloth bodice. Short hooped skirt of red organdie with black fringe and a blue cap with metal cloth front and black lace veil.

Hawaiian Girl—Rainbow colored ribbon streamers over a plain blue skirt and a sleeveless bodice. A lei of vari-colored flowers for the head, a wooden ukelele, a mask and long white stockings.

The three costumes, **without** dolls, nicely displayed in box **$5.00**

Patsy Doll, extra **$3.00**

75

Illustration 74. 13½in (34cm) *Patsy*; all composition; reddish-brown painted hair; brown painted side-glancing eyes, brown painted eyebrows, painted upper eyelashes, a closed mouth; wears a yellow "silk" crepe party dress with four rows of shirring below the bound neck, bound sleeves, two rows of hemstitched ruffles on the skirt, cotton socks, original shoes.

Illustration 75. Advertisement from the 1932 F.A.O. Schwarz Christmas catalog for fancy dress trousseaux for *Patsy*. Russian, Egyptian and Hawaiian costumes were created in the F.A.O. Schwarz studios. Collectors owning these in a trunk set might not realize they were authentic commercial outfits. F.A.O. Schwarz usually offered many child-size costumes such as those for an Indian, cowboy, ballerina and others, and the dolls were not excluded.

Illustration 78. 14in (36cm) *Patsy*; all composition; brown painted hair; brown painted side-glancing eyes, painted upper eyelashes, a closed mouth; wears a white dress opening completely down the back of damask-like material with a square neck and deep hem, matching undergarment, replaced shoes; label in dress reads: "EFFanBEE//DOLL//FINEST & BEST" in an oval and underneath "MADE IN U.S.A.;" doll is marked: "EFFanBEE//PATSY//PAT.PEND.// DOLL." The bloomer dresses such as this were cut a bit shorter than other styles. *Nancy Carlson Collection. Photograph by David Carlson.*

78

Illustration 79. Back view of the 14in (36cm) *Patsy*, seen in *Illustration 78*, showing the label on the back of the dress. *Nancy Carlson Collection. Photograph by David Carlson.*

79

76

77

Illustration 76. 13½in (34cm) *Patsy* from J. C. Penney, dating from the 1930s, models a Molly-'es creation which has a small label sewn inside the neck back marked only with the letter "P." *Judy Johnson Collection.*

Illustration 77. 13½in (34cm) *Patsy*; all composition; red painted hair; blue painted side-glancing eyes, brown painted eyebrows, painted upper eyelashes, a closed mouth; wears original green raincoat with the center closing, two buttons and a belt, matching pieced crown hat with a stitched brim, missing original shoes. There were very few 1930s versions of these dolls with blue painted eyes. They were typical from 1946 to 1949, except for the black versions which had brown eyes. *Arby Rice Collection, courtesy of Ethel Stewart. Photograph by Darryl Dennis.*

Illustration 80. 13½in (34cm) rare Indian *Patsy*; all composition; painted black hair; brown painted side-glancing eyes, black painted eyebrows, painted upper eyelashes; wears her all original cotton outfit which is labeled: "EFFanBEE//DOLL//FINEST & BEST" in an oval and underneath "MADE IN U.S.A." There has been some paint touch-up on the hair, but otherwise she has her original paint with some crazing. The doll was the childhood toy of the owner's friend. *The late Sara Barrett Collection.*

Illustration 81. Back view of the 13½in (34cm) rare Indian *Patsy*, seen in *Illustration 80*, showing the placement of the label which is sewn onto the clothing. *The late Sara Barrett Collection.*

Illustration 82. 13½in (34cm) rare Chinese *Patsy*; all composition; black painted hair with a molded headband; large brown painted eyes with black pupils and two white highlights painted in only half of the eye socket with long eyelashes filling the top half, black painted eyebrows, black painted eyelashes, a closed pink mouth; wears a lined pink brocade jacket trimmed in aqua which is now faded with narrow white braid trim at the neck and sleeves and on the legs of the pants, handmade lined pink brocade slippers with turned toes; marked on torso: "EFFANBEE//PATSY//PAT.PEND.// DOLL;" 1927. The doll was evidently made by Effanbee "to special order." Her hair was professionally sprayed with a stencil for the bangs and she was professionally dressed but her costume has a lot of handwork that would not be done in a factory. *Dorothy Tonkin Collection.*

Illustration 83. Back view of the 13½in (34cm) rare Chinese *Patsy* doll, seen in *Illustration 82*, showing the back of the hair and the marking on the torso. *Dorothy Tonkin Collection.*

80　　　　　　81

Illustration 84. Close-up of the 13½in (34cm) rare Chinese *Patsy* doll, seen in *Illustrations 82 and 83*, showing the detail of the painting of the eyes and the hair. *Dorothy Tonkin Collection.*

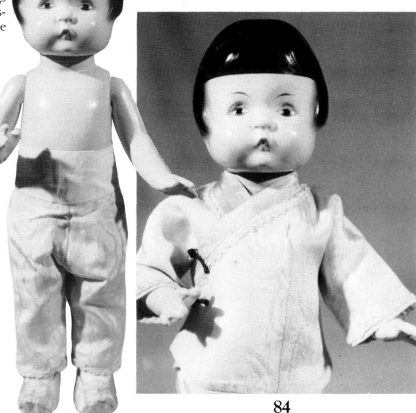

83　　　　　　82　　　　　　84

85

87

Illustration 85. 13½in (34cm) black *Patsy*; all composition; black painted hair; brown painted side-glancing eyes with extra large black pupils, black painted eyebrows, black painted upper eyelashes; wears her original blue batiste dress with lace at the neck and sleeves; marked on the torso: "EFFANBEE//PATSY//PAT.PEND.// DOLL;" 1928.

Illustration 87. 13½in (34cm) black *Patsy Brother*; all composition; black painted hair; brown painted side-glancing eyes, brown painted eyebrows, brown painted upper eyelashes, a closed mouth; wears a blue and white one-piece cotton suit with pearl button trim which opens in the back, original shoes and socks; marked on the torso: "EFFANBEE//PATSY// PAT.PEND.//DOLL;" 1920s. The metal heart-shaped bracelet tag he is wearing has been added as it was not included until 1932. *Joyce Olsen Collection.*

86

88

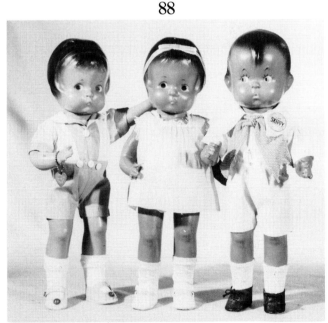

Illustration 86. 13½in (34cm) black *Patsy* (also shown in *Illustration 85*) and 14in (36cm) black *Skippy*; all composition; black painted hair; brown painted side-glancing eyes, black painted eyebrows, black painted upper eyelashes, closed mouths. *Patsy* wears a blue batiste dress over a combination undergarment and replaced shoes and socks while *Skippy* wears a white shirt with a red dotted tie, cream trousers, cotton socks and oxfords. *Skippy, Joyce Olsen Collection.*

Illustration 88. Comparative view of 13½in (34cm) black *Patsy Brother* (seen in *Illustration 87*), 13½in (34cm) black *Patsy* (also seen in *Illustrations 85* and *86*) and 14in (36cm) black *Skippy* (seen in *Illustration 86*). They are all marked on the torso: "EFFANBEE//PATSY//PAT.PEND.//DOLL." *Patsy Brother* and *Skippy, Joyce Olsen Collection.*

89

Illustration 89. 13½in (34cm) black *Patsy* wearing a home-sewn wool jersey coat with brown fur and a matching beret.

90

Illustration 90. Close-up of the 13½in (34cm) black *Patsy*, seen in *Illustration 89*, showing the detail of her beret.

Illustration 91. Advertisement for *Patsy* from the back cover of the F.A.O. Schwarz 1931 Christmas catalog.

91

PATSY TROUSSEAU SUIT CASE

PATSY TROUSSEAU SUIT CASE
No. 222—Tan leather case 14½x10x13 inches with Patsy Doll dressed in organdie dress and cap, including extra dress, underwear, silk pajamas, beach pajamas, coat and hat, slippers and socks $12.75

Illustration 92. 14in (36cm) *Patsy* shown in the F.A.O. Schwarz 1931 Christmas catalog. Wearing her original Effanbee factory dress and hat of organdy, *Patsy* came in a real leather case with additional creations by F.A.O. Schwarz including a dress, underwear, silk pajamas, beach pajamas, a coat and hat and slippers and socks. All this was available for $12.75.

Illustration 95. An example of the markings on the second type of sleep-eyed *Patsy*. By now the company wants there to be no doubt that the doll is "the real thing." The head is marked: "EFFanBEE//PATSY," the torso is marked: "EFFanBEE//PATSY//DOLL." *Photograph by David Carlson.*

PATSY

Here's Patsy herself, all dressed up in her new gingham dress and sunbonnet ready for a week-end visit to the country. She certainly is cute, isn't she? Patsy is always ready for a good time with you, ready to laugh, play, sing with you. She's really a wonderful companion.

Patsy with real hair wearing her smartly tailored velvet coat and hat

94

Illustration 93. Volume 1, Number 3 of *The Patsytown News*, "A Newspaper For Your Doll," showed this *Patsy* in 1934. By this time she came with the metal heart-shaped bracelet tag and the gold paper heart-shaped tag. *Marlene Wendt Collection.*

Illustration 94. Volume 1, Number 3 of *The Patsytown News*, "A Newspaper For Your Doll," also showed this *Patsy* in 1934. This 13½in (34cm) to 14in (36cm) *Patsy* would be all composition. Her wig could come in blonde, brownette or red and could be either mohair or human hair. She could have sleep eyes and at this time would come with a metal heart-shaped bracelet tag and the gold paper heart-shaped tag. This *Patsy* is shown wearing a velvet coat with full gathers and a matching cloche hat with flower trim. *Marlene Wendt Collection.*

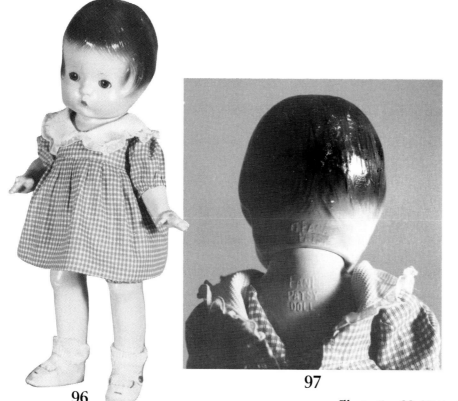

Illustration 96. 13½in (34cm) *Patsy*; all composition; brown painted hair; brown sleep eyes, brown painted eyebrows, real upper eyelashes and painted upper and lower eyelashes, a closed mouth; wears a blue and white checked print dress with a piqué collar trimmed with a ruffle of organdy; marked on the head: "EFFanBEE// PATSY," marked on the torso: "EFFanBEE//PATSY//DOLL;" 1930s. *Nancy Carlson Collection. Photograph by David Carlson.*

Illustration 97. Back view of the 13½ in (34cm) *Patsy*, seen in *Illustration 96*, showing the marking on the back of the neck and the torso. *Nancy Carlson Collection. Photograph by David Carlson.*

97

96

Illustration 98. 13½in (34cm) *Patsy*; all composition; reddish-brown painted hair; brown sleep eyes, brown painted eyebrows, painted and real hair upper eyelashes, painted lower eyelashes, closed mouth; wears her all-original blouse and panties combination with an organdy-trimmed collar hemstitched in red, a separate red and white pleated cotton print skirt, white piqué bonnet which matches the blouse, red satin bow at the neck, silk socks and red shoes; 1930s. *Judy Berry Collection. Photograph by Judy Berry.*

Illustration 99. Close-up of the 13½in (34cm) *Patsy*, seen in *Illustration 98*, showing the detail of the face and the sleep eyes. *Judy Berry Collection. Photograph by Judy Berry.*

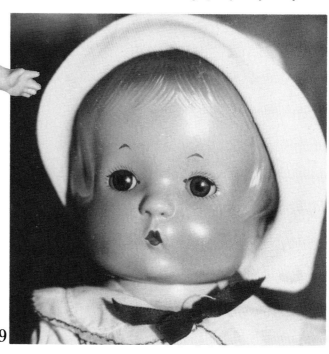

98　　　　**99**

Illustration 103. Close-up of the 13½in (34cm) rare mulatto *Patsy*, seen in *Illustrations 101* and *102*, showing the detail of the face and the glassene eyes. *Peggy Yale Collection. Photograph by Laureen Pharr.*

103

102

Illustration 100. 13½in (34cm) *Patsy*, seen in *Illustrations 98* and *99*, with her original box which shows four poses from the early *Patsy* publicity plus a head view of *Bubbles*, the Effanbee baby doll sensation with her finger in her mouth. *Judy Berry Collection. Photograph by Judy Berry.*

Illustration 102. Close-up of the 13½in (34cm) rare mulatto *Patsy*, seen in *Illustration 101*, showing the detail of the face as well as the embroidery work on the collar of the dress. *Peggy Yale Collection. Photograph by Laureen Pharr.*

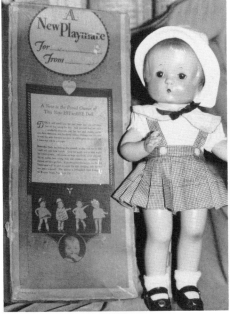

100

101

Illustration 101. 13½in (34cm) rare mulatto *Patsy*; all composition; black painted hair; brown glassene sleep eyes, brown painted single-stroke eyebrows, painted and real hair upper eyelashes, painted lower eyelashes, a closed mouth; wears a blue organdy dress and bonnet with hemstitching on the ruffles and collar which has a hand-embroidered pink blossom with blue leaves and embroidery work with pink ribbon pulled through the openings. She is a light chocolate color. *Peggy Yale Collection. Photograph by Laureen Pharr.*

104

105

Illustration 105. 13½in (34cm) *Patsy*; all composition; brown painted hair; green sleep eyes, brown painted eyebrows, painted and real hair upper eyelashes, painted lower eyelashes, a closed mouth; wears a green cotton print dress with a wide organdy collar trimmed in machine stitching, replaced shoes; dress has a woven gold and red label on a white background reading: "EFFanBEE//DURABLE//DOLLS" inside a heart and underneath "MADE IN U.S.A.;" 1930s.

Illustration 106. 13½in (34cm) *Patsy*; all composition; dark red mohair wig over molded hair; brown sleep eyes, brown painted eyebrows, painted and real hair upper eyelashes, painted lower eyelashes, a closed mouth; wears a green silk dress with a hand-embroidered motif of pink and gold on a deep yoke with a gathered skirt, matching turned-back brim bonnet with ribbon ties, replaced shoes; dress has a woven gold and red label on a white background reading: "EFFanBEE//DURABLE//DOLLS" inside a heart and underneath "MADE IN U.S.A.;" 1930s.

Illustration 104. 13½in (34cm) *Patsy*; all composition; brown painted hair; blue sleep eyes, brown painted eyebrows, painted and real hair upper eyelashes, painted lower eyelashes, a closed mouth; wears a specialty shop party dress of pale blue organdy with six tucks on the yoke, hemstitched ruffles in a jacket effect and on the sleeves at the edges and the bottom of the hem, full skirt with tucks and a hemstitched ruffle, replaced shoes and socks; circa 1930s. *Gerrie Lee Collection.*

Illustration 107. Back view of the 13½ in (34cm) *Patsy*, seen in *Illustration 106*, showing the placement of the label on the dress.

106

107

PATSY TROUSSEAU

PATSY TROUSSEAU

No. 26/13—Patsy's very stylish new suitcase that will carry the doll and all her things. The case, 15" x 10" x 4½", is shiny ribbed black patent leatherette very strongly made, nicely lined and finished with bright nickeled trim, lock and key. Patsy, 13" tall fits in nicely and wears a pretty dotted dress, a combination, shoes and socks. In the suitcase are her "extras"— another dress and hat, fancy pajamas, also beach pajamas and a big floppy sun hat, another pantie dress for play and a very smart coat and matching hat made of stylish flannel. There's a comb too to curl her pretty real hair, also soap, sponge and a washcloth. Patsy of almost unbreakable composition, head and limbs. Complete.....................................**$15.00**

108

Illustration 108. Deluxe trousseau set offered by F.A.O. Schwarz in its 1935 Christmas catalog. The garment the doll is shown wearing was the one she came in from the Effanbee factory. The special "extra" outfits were created in the F.A.O. Schwarz studios.

Finger Nailed Patsy

Finger-Nailed Patsy—Another contradiction to the oft repeated remark that "Dolls haven't changed much." Each year those interested in dolls have found changes and improvements in construction, material or design and in the closer resemblance to the "real." And so this year another added feature—actual fingernails that can be polished and cared for—a vital fact in the estimation of thousands of young girls. A small piece of curved, colorless celluloid inserted in the cuticles of the five fingers—simple yet very realistic. With a pretty head of real human curly hair these dolls look sweet in their dainty plaid dresses. They wear a little pantie combination and white socks and slippers. Strong composition body, movable arms, legs and head with sleeping eyes.

No. 25/191—Patsy, 13 inches $4.25
No. 25/192—Patsy Joan, 16 inches 5.00
No. 25/193—Patsy Ann, 19 inches 7.75

110

109

Illustration 109. 13½in (34cm) *Patsy*; all composition; painted red hair; green sleep eyes, painted brown eyebrows, painted and real hair upper eyelashes, painted lower eyelashes, a closed mouth; wears a blue and white cotton outfit with pearl button trim, a combination undergarment, replaced shoes and socks. *Arby Rice Collection, courtesy of Ethel Stewart. Photograph by Darryl Dennis.*

Illustration 110. Manufacturers were apparently always endeavoring to come up with something "new and different" as is indicated with this advertisement from the F.A.O. Schwarz 1936 Christmas catalog for a *Patsy* with fingernails. "Real" fingernails of curved colorless celluloid inserted in the cuticles of the five fingers were highly advertised, yet only two examples have been found. These are not to be confused with the indented and painted-on finger tips on the composition. The celluloid fingernails actually protruded a bit beyond the finger tip.

111

112

Illustration 112. Back view of the 13½in (34cm) *Tousle Head* (a *Patsy* variant), seen in *Illustration 111*, showing the placement of the label on the jumper. *Ruth Douglas Collection.*

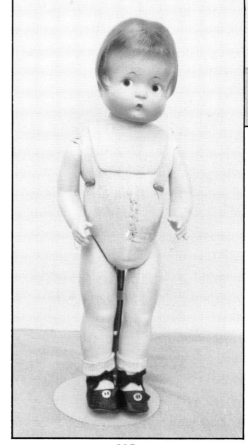

114

Illustration 111. 13½in (34cm) all original *Tousle Head*, a *Patsy* variant; tousled fur wig; brown sleep eyes, brown painted eyebrows, painted and real hair upper eyelashes, painted lower eyelashes, a closed mouth; wears a blouse and panties sewn together as a combination suit, red print jumper with dotted squares and leaves which matches the beret and the panties, red striped socks, red shoes; dress has a woven gold and red label reading: "EFFanBEE//DURABLE//DOLLS" inside a heart; 1933 to 1934. A factory "put-together," this doll has a *Patsy Babykin* head while the rest of the body is from a *Patsy* mold. This was an attempt to create something "different." A few other variant combinations were tried by the company. *Ruth Douglas Collection.*

Illustration 113. 15½in (39cm) *Patsy*; composition head on a separate composition shoulder plate, cloth body, composition arms and legs; brown painted hair; brown painted side-glancing eyes, brown painted eyebrows, painted upper eyelashes, a closed mouth; marked on the back of the neck: "EFFANBEE//PATSY," no marking on the shoulder plate; 1936. *Marianne Gardiner Collection. Photograph by Polly Judd.*

Illustration 114. Back view of the 15½in (39cm) *Patsy*, seen in *Illustration 113*, showing the body construction and the marked head with the separate unmarked shoulder piece. *Marianne Gardiner Collection. Photograph by Polly Judd.*

113

Illustration 115. Close-up of the 15½in (39cm) *Patsy*, seen in *Illustrations 113* and *114* showing the marking on the back of the neck. *Marianne Gardiner Collection. Photograph by Polly Judd.*

115

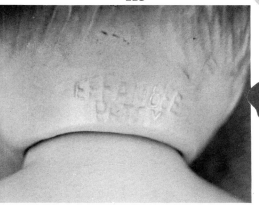

Illustration 117. 15½in (39cm) *Patsy*; composition head on a separate composition shoulder plate, cloth body, composition arms and legs; brown painted hair; brown painted side-glancing eyes, brown painted eyebrows, painted upper eyelashes, a closed mouth; wears a tan-colored ten-gallon hat, red cotton blouse and panties, green neckerchief, brown suede-like jacket with tan trim and metal studs, brown suede-like skirt with tan fringe trim, holster with gun, original socks and black tie shoes; marked on the back of the neck: "EFFANBEE/PATSY;" 1936. This doll was part of the regular Effanbee line for 1936 but some of the *Skippy* dolls and this version of *Patsy* were designated *Texas Centennial* dolls with silver circular stickers on the hats. *Mary Lu Trowbridge Collection. Photograph by Mary Lu Trowbridge.*

117

116

Illustration 116. 15½in (39cm) *Patsy*, seen in *Illustrations 113, 114* and *115*, shown fully dressed in her cowgirl outfit consisting of a tan-colored ten-gallon hat, a red cotton blouse and panties, neckerchief, brown suede-like jacket with tan trim and metal studs, brown suede-like skirt with tan fringe trim, original socks and black tie shoes. *Marianne Gardiner Collection. Photograph by Polly Judd.*

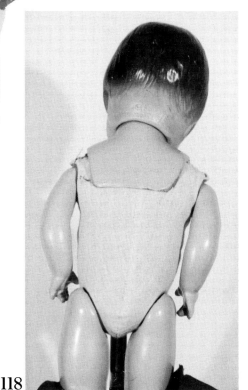

118

Illustration 118. Close-up of the 15½in (39cm) *Patsy*, seen in *Illustration 117*, showing the body construction and the marking on the back of the neck. *Mary Lu Trowbridge Collection. Photograph by Mary Lu Trowbridge.*

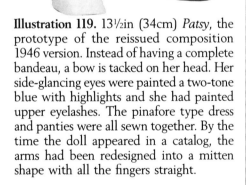

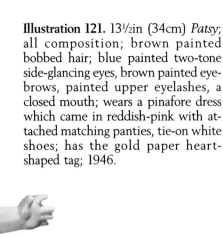

Illustration 121. 13½in (34cm) *Patsy*; all composition; brown painted bobbed hair; blue painted two-tone side-glancing eyes, brown painted eyebrows, painted upper eyelashes, a closed mouth; wears a pinafore dress which came in reddish-pink with attached matching panties, tie-on white shoes; has the gold paper heart-shaped tag; 1946.

121

119

Illustration 119. 13½in (34cm) *Patsy*, the prototype of the reissued composition 1946 version. Instead of having a complete bandeau, a bow is tacked on her head. Her side-glancing eyes were painted a two-tone blue with highlights and she had painted upper eyelashes. The pinafore type dress and panties were all sewn together. By the time the doll appeared in a catalog, the arms had been redesigned into a mitten shape with all the fingers straight.

Illustration 120. Page from the 1946 Effanbee catalog showing the redesigned 13½in (34cm) *Patsy*, at the top left, with a full red ribbon bandeau around her hair, different arms and wearing gripper snap roller skates. Her garment is described as red but it was actually rather pinkish. She was not marked at all but came with a gold paper heart-shaped tag. The *Patsy Joan*, shown here at the top right, is marked "EFFANDBEE" (with the "D" added), not "EFFANBEE" as in earlier years. The significance of the variation in the spelling change at this time on various dolls is unknown.

120

LEFT: Color Illustration 34. *Patsy Ann* wearing a printed piqué coat trimmed with felt with piqué collar, cuffs and pockets and a matching bonnet with a felt brim and streamer ties. *Inge Simms Collection.*

ABOVE: Color Illustration 35. *Patsy Ann*, seen in *Color Illustration 34*, shown with her original box. *Inge Simms Collection.*

OPPOSITE PAGE: Color Illustration 36. Close-up of the *Patsy Ann*, seen in *Color Illustrations 34* and *35*. *Inge Simms Collection.*

Back view of the *Patsy
Ann*, seen in *Color Illustra-
tion 37*, with her trunk. *Edell
Lashley Collection.*

**FAR RIGHT: Color Illustra-
tion 39.** *Patsy Ann*, seen in
Color Illustrations 37 and *38*,
wearing a snowsuit and helmet with zippered snow
boots from the wardrobe in
the trunk. *Edell Lashley Collection.*

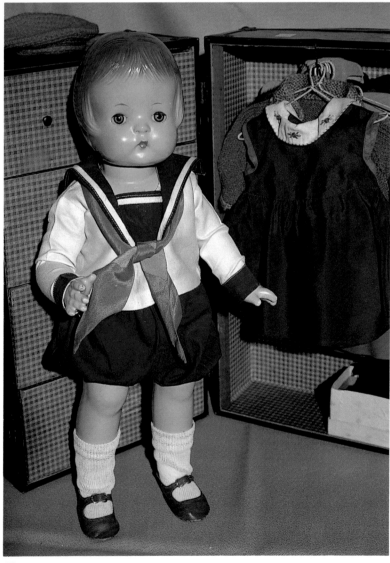

LEFT: Color Illustration 37. *Patsy Ann* with a
trunk and extensive wardrobe. She is modeling
a handmade outfit consisting of a middy blouse
and gym bloomers. *Edell Lashley Collection.*

ABOVE: Color Illustration 40. *Patsy Ann*, seen
in *Color Illustrations 37, 38* and *39*, wearing a
handmade smocked party dress from the wardrobe in the trunk. *Edell Lashley Collection.*

Color Illustration 41. *Patsy Ann* wearing a specialty shop frock and hat. *Jackie Rovick Collection.*

BELOW: Color Illustration 42. *Patsy Ann* wearing a sweater and green flannel pleated skirt and beret. *Jean Millen Collection.*

RIGHT: Color Illustration 43. *Patsy Ann* modeling a blue and white cotton party dress with a pleated skirt.

ABOVE: Color Illustration 44. Side view of the *Patsy Ann,* seen in *Color Illustration 43.*

Color Illustration 45. All-original *Patsy Ann* in a yellow silk party frock and matching bonnet by Effanbee. *Nancy Carlson Collection. Photograph by David Carlson.*

All-original *Patsy Ann* with a human hair wig wearing a blue organdy party dress by Effanbee. *Inge Simms Collection.*

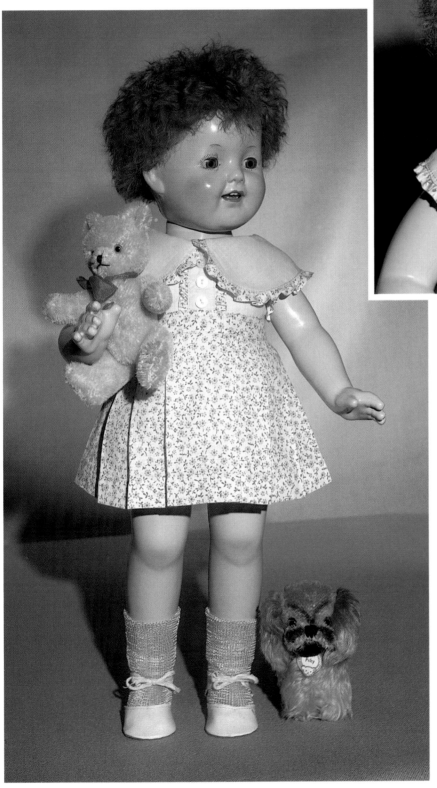

LEFT: Color Illustration 47. A *Patsy Ann* variant usually advertised in the toy catalogs as simply *"Tousel Head"* but actually named *Betty Brite*.

ABOVE: Color Illustration 48. Close-up of the *Patsy Ann* variant, seen in *Color Illustration 47.*

OPPOSITE PAGE: Color Illustration 49. *Patsy Ann* variant *Betty Brite* with the typical marked torso, the *Lovums* type head and the tousle wig. *Patsy Moyer Collection. Photograph by Patsy Moyer.*

BELOW: Color Illustration 50. *Patsy Ann* variant with a marked *Patsy Ann* body. This was Effanbee's *Shirley Temple* type.

ABOVE: Color Illustration 51. *Patsy Ann* in an all-original party frock and bonnet by Effanbee. *Jackie Rovick Collection.*

RIGHT: Color Illustration 52. Side view of the *Patsy Ann,* seen in *Color Illustration 51. Jackie Rovick Collection.*

RIGHT: Color Illustration 53. *Patsy Ann* in specialty shop beach pajamas from a trunk set with a wardrobe. *Jackie Rovick Collection.*

ABOVE: Color Illustration 54. *Patsy Ann* in a specialty shop cotton outfit from a trunk set with a wardrobe. *Jackie Rovick Collection.*

RIGHT: Color Illustration 55. *Patsy Ann* in a specialty shop dress with a trunk set showing the wardrobe, selections of which can also be seen in *Color Illustrations 53* and *54. Jackie Rovick Collection.*

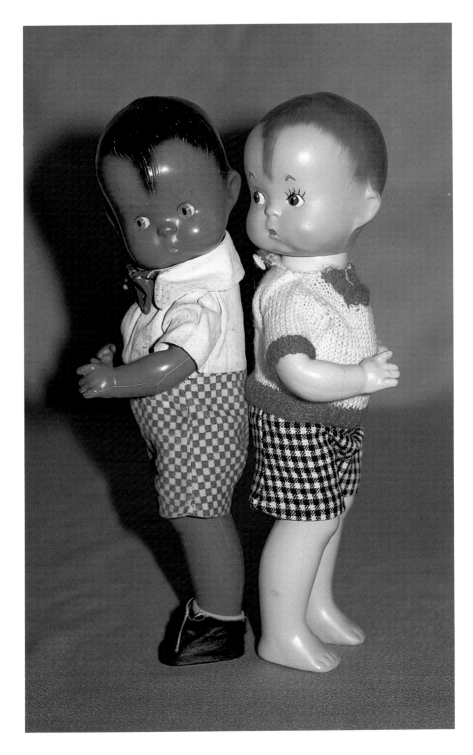

LEFT: **Color Illustration 56.** All-original all-composition *Skippy* dolls in black and white versions.

BELOW: **Color Illustration 57.** The redesigned *Skippy* with a cloth torso. *Nancy Carlson Collection. Photograph by David Carlson.*

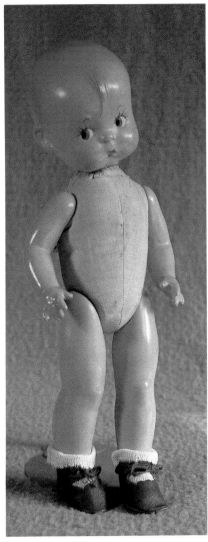

BELOW: Color Illustration 58. All-original *Skippy* with labeled clothing. *Nancy Carlson Collection. Photograph by David Carlson.*

RIGHT: Color Illustration 59. Close-up of the all-original *Skippy,* seen in *Color Illustration 58. Nancy Carlson Collection. Photograph by David Carlson.*

RIGHT: Color Illustration 60. Back view of the all-original *Skippy,* seen in *Color Illustrations 58* and *59,* showing the Effanbee label with the NRA symbol. *Nancy Carlson Collection. Photograph by David Carlson.*

LEFT: **Color Illustration 61.** Comparative view of the first *Skippy* in a rare black version with a rare black *Patsy Twin Brother* in original clothes. *Skippy, Joyce Olsen Collection.*

BELOW: **Color Illustration 62.** The second version of the cloth-bodied *Skippy* in his original clothing and with his original box. *Patsy Moyer Collection. Photograph by Patsy Moyer.*

Color Illustration 63. A rare *Boy Scout Skippy* with composition molded shoes and green socks shown with a later issue *Skippy Soldier* in a World War II uniform.

361ME—Patsy: 13½" doll. Striped novelty cloth dress, flare sleeves, lace trim braid on shoulder and yoke. Ribbon bow for head. Fully jointed. Moving eyes and eyelashes. Shoes and socks. Individually packaged in display box. 2 doz. to carton.

122

Illustration 122. The 1949 Effanbee catalog shows 13½in (34cm) *Patsy* dolls with the gold paper heart-shaped tags and wearing pinafore dresses.

124

Illustration 124. 14in (36cm) *Patsy*; all composition; brown painted hair; blue painted eyes, brown painted eyebrows, painted upper eyelashes, a closed mouth. This advertisement appeared in the 1947 Montgomery Ward catalog which was the only source for the doll with a cap matching its dress rather than a hair ribbon. She was described as a "dainty and lovable little girl doll made of hard-to-break composition, nicely molded...Dressed in checked cotton dress with panty attached."

Illustration 123. 13½in (34cm) *Patsy*; all composition; brown painted hair; blue painted side-glancing eyes, brown painted eyebrows, painted upper eyelashes, a closed mouth; wears a pinafore dress of pink and white checked cotton with red eyelet trim on the shoulders, red trim at the hem top, silk socks, slippers, a red hair bow tacked on her head; no markings on the doll; gold paper heart-shaped tag reads: "This is//PATSY//The Lovable Imp//with tiltable head//and movable limb//AN//EFFanBEE//DURABLE// DOLL;" 1946 to 1949. She is shown in her original box. *Lenore Coughlin Collection.*

Illustration 125. 14in (36cm) *Patsy* as advertised in the January 1948 issue of *Children's Activities* magazine. She came with white tie-on shoes and gripper snap red roller skate shoes. She was available for $3.10, postpaid.

PATSY DOLL. She's lovable, she's adorable, she's petite. This EFFan-BEE doll, famous before the war, is even cuter now with her new checked pink and white gingham pinafore trimmed in red with panties to match. White shoes and socks and red hair ribbon. One of the nicest features about Patsy is her satin-smooth skin finish which gives a most lifelike effect. This, along with her piquant face and bright blue eyes makes her a most charming doll. 14" tall. The versatility of Patsy has now been extended with the addition of real **roller** skates to her wardrobe. These skates can be readily interchanged with her regular shoes since the skates are the shoe type. **Price, postpaid, $3.10.**

123   **125**

Illustration 126. 13½in (34cm) *Patsy* dolls shown in the 1949 Effanbee doll catalog. Note the original box and the gold paper heart-shaped tags. There were no gold metal heart-shaped bracelet tags at this time.

311—Patsy: 13 ½" doll all composition. Jointed arms and legs. Head turns in any direction. Attractive cotton dress and panties. Bright ribbon bow. White shoes and socks. Individually packaged in display box. 2 doz. to carton.

126

127

Illustration 127. 13½in (34cm) black *Patsy*; all composition; black painted hair; brown painted side-glancing (to the left) eyes, black painted eyebrows, painted upper eyelashes, a closed mouth; wears a blue and white checked rayon dress with touches of red trim on the collar and waist, replaced shoes; no markings on the doll. Some black models were part of the actual line at this time and were not just made "to special order."

Illustration 128. This advertisement from an unnamed Seattle, Washington, newspaper for December 1, 1946, lists *Patsy* as 14in (36cm) tall and shows inaccurate artwork with both arms bent. The copy reads: "Patsy dolls are back for little girls to mother! All composition with tiltable head and movable limbs." She was available for $3.25.

OPPOSITE PAGE: Illustration 129. Advertisement from an unnamed Seattle, Washington, newspaper for December 6, 1946, lists *Patsy* as 13½in (34cm) tall and the caption describes her as "Dressed in a polka dot pinafore with bright red ribbon headband." Sizes listed in advertising often differ on the same doll as can be seen with this advertisement and the one shown in *Illustration 128*.

"Patsy" dolls are back for little girls to mother! All composition with tiltable head and movable limbs. 14" high.

3.25

• *Toyland.*

128

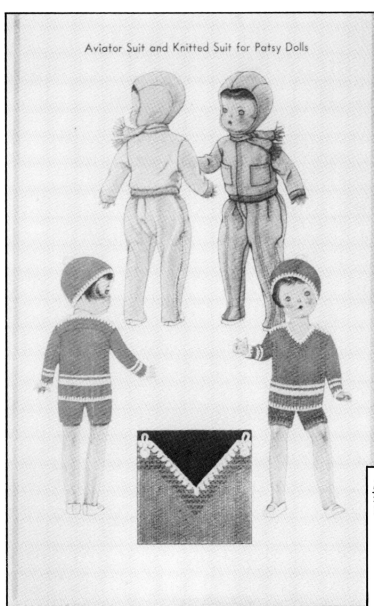

Aviator Suit and Knitted Suit for Patsy Dolls

M°CALL PRINTED PATTERN

Illustration 130. The envelope front from McCall printed pattern number 45 for 14in (36cm) *Patsy* dolls. The two outfits — an aviator suit and a knitted suit of a pullover sweater, short pants and a beret — were for *Patsy's* twin brother.

Illustration 131. The envelope front from Butterick pattern number 437 for 14in (36cm) *Patsy* and similar dolls. The patterns were for a coat and beret for brother and sister, a suit for brother and a romper frock for sister. The romper frock is the typical combination suit which *Patsy* wore with a matching sleeveless dress over it.

130

131

PATSY—the lovable Effanbee Doll. Dressed in a polka dot pinafore with bright red ribbon headband. 13½ inches high, molded hair, movable arms, legs and head.

$2.98

129

"Sew-Easy" Doll Patterns

Fit

PATSY DOLLS

or any Doll of same size (14 inches)

COMPLETE PATTERNS FOR THE EIGHT PICTURED GARMENTS

DRESS NO. 2

TEDDIES NO. 8

HAT NO. 7

BONNET NO. 6

DRESS NO. 1

COAT NO. 4

BERET NO. 5

(CUT ON OUTSIDE LINE)

BEACH PAJAMAS NO. 3

These patterns are the exact duplicate of those used by the maker of the finest ready-made and SEW-EASY Already-Cut-To-Sew-Doll-Clothes and if accurately followed are warranted to fit.

ACCURATE ENOUGH FOR AN ADULT

SIMPLE ENOUGH FOR A CHILD

Copyright 1931 by Sonia Alch

132

Illustration 133. The envelope front for Butterick pattern number 445 which features a wardrobe for *Patsy* consisting of a fur-trimmed coat and matching hat, a ruffled party dress and hat, a sailor style dress, pajamas, a slip and a combination undergarment.

445

BUTTERICK

PATTERN
INCLUDING THE
NEW DELTOR
25c

WARDROBE
FOR PATSY
DOLL

Consisting of Coat, Two
Dresses, Slip, Combination,
Pajamas and Two Hats.

a Delineator Style

133

Illustration 132. "Sew-Easy" doll patterns for *Patsy*, copyright 1931 by Sonia Alch, made by M. and S. Alch, Berkeley, California, featured patterns for two dresses, a teddy, a bonnet, a hat, a coat, a beret and beach pajamas. The copy reads: "These patterns are the exact duplicate of those used by the maker of the finest ready-made and SEW-EASY Already-Cut-To-Sew-Doll-Clothes and if accurately followed are warranted to fit."

Illustration 134. The envelope front for Butterick pattern number 442 for a wardrobe for *Patsy* consisting of a party dress, a pleated skirt and blouse, a coat with a cape collar, pajamas, a bathing suit, a hat, a beret and a combination slip and step-in. Some of the recommended materials were crepe de chine, taffeta, organdy, lawn or dotted swiss. Note that the artist has carefully drawn the metal heart-shaped bracelet tag on the doll's right arm.

442

LENGTH OF DOLL 14 INCH

BUTTERICK PATTERN

25c
30c. in Canada

A
DELINEATOR STYLE
INCLUDING THE
NEW DELTOR

WARDROBE
FOR PATSY DOLL

Consisting of Two Dresses,
Hat, Beret, Coat, Pajamas,
Bathing Suit and Combina-
tion Slip and Step-In

134

Chapter Four

Skippy,

Percy L. Crosby's Creation

Skippy was just one year behind *Patsy* in arriving on the Effanbee doll scene. *Toys and Novelties* magazine for February 29, 1929, carried one of the first announcements:

"The latest addition to the popular *Fleischaker and Baum* line of dolls is Patsy's new 'boy friend' Skippy, modeled after the famous Skippy of Percy Crosby's clever cartoon. Skippy is a cute little rascal and a suitable companion for Patsy. Patsy, herself, holds her popularity, and this year is fitted out with a big variety of new costumes."

Illustration 135. Advertisement from the June 1929 issue of *Toy World* magazine showing the original version of *Skippy* with the *Patsy* body marked: "EFFanBEE//PATSY//PAT.PEND.// DOLL." The doll has a harmonica in his pocket and carries a miniature "Skippy" book. He wears a brocade type white shirt which is similar to an early *Patsy* dress, a tie with the Effanbee button with the heart emblem on it, felt trousers and *Patsy* type shoes and socks. **135**

FOR CHILDREN'S DAY
The Famous Mischievous
SKIPPY!

June, 1929

Millions of children and parents follow with delight the antics and adventures of Skippy in the leading newspapers and magazines of the country. This perfect doll reproduction of Skippy will make an instant appeal to them. He will equal Patsy's popularity.

We have secured the exclusive rights for doll reproduction of Skippy from his creator, Percy Crosby.

FLEISCHAKER & BAUM
Originators of Doll Hits and Makers of Quality Dolls

Office and Factory: 45 Greene Street, New York

Salesrooms: 45 East 17th Street, New York

"OF COURSE IT'S AN EFFANBEE DOLL"

Please mention **TOY WORLD** *when writing to advertisers*

136

Seven costumes were illustrated for *Skippy* — a cowboy, a farmer boy in long overalls, two styles of short-sleeved shirts with a belt and short trousers, a baseball uniform and what appears to be a military uniform as well as a shirt with a tie and long trousers. These were for the full composition doll.

By June, *Toy World* magazine carried a full-page advertisement which illustrated a full-length *Skippy*. The copy read: "For Children's Day//The Famous Mischievous//SKIPPY." Original artwork of the original cartoon character Skippy, carrying a book and doffing his cap, is also included. The copy read:

"Millions of children and parents follow with delight the antics and adventures of Skippy in the leading newspapers and magazines of the country. This perfect doll reproduction of Skippy will make an instant appeal to them. He will equal Patsy's popularity.

"We have secured the exclusive rights for doll reproduction of Skippy from his creator, Percy Crosby.

"FLEISCHAKER & BAUM, Originators of Doll Hits and Makers of Quality Dolls."

137

Illustration 136. 13½in (34cm) *Skippy*; all composition; blonde painted hair; blue painted side-glancing eyes, brown painted eyebrows, five painted upper eyelashes for each eye, a closed mouth; wears a white brocade type shirt with a woven design, a blue and white striped bow tie, a brown belt with a buckle, blue cotton short trousers with button trim on the sides; marked on the back of the neck: "EFFANBEE//SKIPPY//©//P.L. CROSBY," marked on the body: "EFFanBEE//PATSY//PAT.PEND.// DOLL;" shirt has a printed red and white cloth label sewn into the neck seam which reads: "EFFanBEE// DOLL//FINEST & BEST" in red in an oval and underneath "MADE IN U.S.A." in red; 1929. This costume is one of the first seven costumes shown in *Playthings* magazine in May 1929. The other six original costumes were for a cowboy, a farmer boy, a baseball uniform with removable two-tone shoes, an open-necked shirt with a tie and long trousers, the same with short trousers and a soldier boy with puttees. *Evelyn Sharratt Collection. Photograph by Mary Lu Trowbridge.*

Illustration 137. Close-up of the 13½in (34cm) *Skippy*, seen in *Illustration 136*, showing the detail of the face and the clothes. *Evelyn Sharratt Collection. Photograph by Mary Lu Trowbridge.*

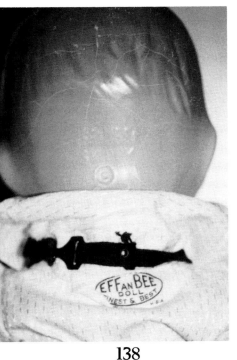

Illustration 138. Back view of the 13½ in (34cm) *Skippy*, seen in *Illustrations 136* and *137*, showing the marking on the back of the neck and the placement of the label on the shirt. *Evelyn Sharratt Collection. Photograph by Mary Lu Trowbridge.*

138

In this first full-page advertisement, *Skippy* is wearing short felt trousers with a long-sleeved shirt pushed up on one arm. The insignia button on his tie has a gold heart on a red background with "EFFANBEE" in the center of the heart. The body appears to be exactly the same as that of *Patsy*. Even the shoes are the same. This is, no doubt, a prototype prepared before much of the wardrobe was designed. In his pocket was a small harmonica and he held a small booklet (which has never yet been discovered) entitled "Skippy."

Within a short period of time, a button was designed especially for *Skippy*. It read: "EFFANBEE//DOLLS//I AM//SKIPPY//TRADE MARK//THE REAL AMERICAN BOY."

Good Housekeeping magazine had a *Skippy* ready to mail for Christmas 1929. Rather than have him wear little boy clothes, he is dressed as a cowboy, with his hat and neckerchief, long trousers and chaps with three-button trim on each leg. A basic *Skippy* sold for $2.95. This more elaborate costume raised the price to $3.50.

In 1932, and probably earlier, F.A.O. Schwarz offered *Skippy* as a cowboy in a more deluxe tan suede leather outfit studded with nickel. The shirt was white with a black tie. One could order the suit alone for $1.25 and a ten-gallon hat was also available for $.75. Some of these outfits have ended up on *Patsy* in childish play but her equivalent would have been that of a cowgirl.

In June 1931, a full-page advertisement ran in *Playthings* magazine showing a photograph of a shop window filled with *Skippy* dolls in among large posters of child actor Jackie Cooper, who is not named. The headline is: "Skippy Is NOW In The Movies." All the *Skippy* dolls appear to be wearing little boy clothing. The copy declared:

> "The American public is now Skippy conscious. Over 4½ million people have already seen the marvelous Skippy talking picture all through the United States.
>
> "Skippy dolls are made *solely* by Fleischaker & Baum by arrangements with Percy Crosby, his creator. They are extremely lifelike reproductions of Skippy himself. They come in a great variety of costumes and are priced right to sell on sight."

The June 1932 *Toys and Novelties* magazine showed a different display of large Jackie Cooper cutouts, posters and scenes from the movie intermingled with *Skippy* dolls. Short or long pants with bow ties at the necks, plus caps or two-toned "beanies" completed the costumes. The department store was Keith's Inc. in Greenville, South Carolina, in cooperation with the Carolina Theatre. This same store has been mentioned as having *Patsy* parties.

The August 1940 *Playthings* magazine brought the first mention of "Effanbee Dolls With Magnetic Hands...The new Effanbee doll with magnetic hands has made a decided hit." This is the doll with the magic hands which picks up, holds and carries lightweight articles such as household utensils, traveling bags and many other items. These dolls were made in six styles, two of which are shown in the accompanying illustration and they retailed from $2.95 to $4.95 each. An appropriate set of miniature playthings was included with each doll.

Mrs. Alice Crawford of New York is said to have invented the idea of embedding a magnet into the hands of a doll so it could appear to hold small metal-bound objects. An F.A.O. Schwarz toy buyer is said to have favored her idea.

It has been published that the Schwarz firm altered Effanbee dolls and those from other makers and painted over the magnet. This is most certainly in error. In September 1940, *Playthings* magazine carried a top half-page advertisement for "The Dolls With Magnetic Hands and Accesso-

Illustration 139. Advertisement from a 1929 *Good Housekeeping* magazine for a 14in (36cm) *Skippy*, an all-composition doll shown in a cowboy outfit by Effanbee. The doll no longer wears *Patsy* slippers but has tie oxfords. He also wears a *Skippy* pin. The price was $3.50.

ries." Shown in the advertisement are Effanbee's *Little Lady* and *Skippy Sailor*. The copy reads:

"This novelty toy is protected by the following United States Patents: No. 2,213,901 and No. 1,551,050. Licenses have been granted to: (1) F. A. O. Schwarz, 745 Fifth Avenue, New York, N. Y. (Exclusive in Greater New York for 1940.) (2) Fleischaker & Baum, 200 Fifth Avenue, New York, N. Y. No other firms have been licensed under these patents. Dealers and manufacturers will be held strictly accountable for any infringements. Address all inquiries to: W. C. Crawford, 292 Madison Avenue, New York, N. Y."

A separate box at the bottom half of the same page reads:

"See Effanbee's Sensationally NEW Doll With Magnetic Hands. Another new Effanbee smash hit! A beautiful doll with magic hands that can actually pick up, hold and carry lightweight articles.

"Here's a new play idea in dolls, if ever there was one! A really magnetic sales maker. Made in six styles, to retail at $2.95 and $4.95 each. A set of playthings is included with each doll. Get a sample right away — display it — watch how quickly the idea takes with your customers. Write us today. Fleischaker and Baum 200 Fifth Avenue, New York, N. Y."

If the Schwarz company was the first to have the dolls, they probably went to Effanbee to arrange to have them determine *how* to manufacture the dolls with magnets in their hands. It is highly unlikely that the Schwarz firm could punch out the slender doll hands after they had already been painted. There would have been many a broken doll. It is possible, however, that one or two dolls were done experimentally in order to present the idea to Effanbee. These magnetic hand dolls, when found in mint condition, show no sign of being painted over or altered in any way.

Later notices of other licenses for additional companies have not been found, but there appear to have been some.

The F.A.O. Schwarz 1941 Christmas catalog featured *Suzanne*, *Skippy Soldier* and *Skippy Sailor*. The catalog reads:

"Introduced last year, these famous dolls have so endeared themselves to us and our family of little customers that we're featuring them again and some brand new ones too. Whether it's Skippy Sailor signaling to sea, Skippy Soldier beating his drum, or Babykin holding her own bottle we know of no dolls so humanly appealing. A permanent magnet concealed inside the hand enables them to hold metalized toys and so does the trick."

F.A.O. Schwarz stated that it had prepared four different doll assortments of magnetic toys, which are not included in the price of the doll but listed separately.

For *Soldier Skippy*, in khaki clothes at $3.00, there was a drum and sticks, a bugle, binoculars, a flag and a whistle for $1.25. For *Sailor Skippy*, in his regulation middy uniform and hat at $3.00, there was a duffel bag, a pair of signal flags, a scrub pail with a brush and a mop for only $.75.

It is rare for these magnetic hand dolls to be found with even one of the original toys as they were small and easily became lost. Some items were all metal and others were wood with a piece of metal clamped into the item to attach to the magnet in the doll's hand.

The first year for the molded shoes and socks for the *Sailor* and *Soldier* was 1940. However, a rare 1936 *Boy Scout* doll with olive green painted socks and a *Baseball Skippy* with molded painted white socks were earlier. Because of World War II, these dolls were redesigned as military figures. They appear to have been very popular, no doubt with adults as well as children.

A news photograph for November 1942 showed a young girl saluting *Soldier* and *Sailor Skippy* and *WAAC* and *WAVE Suzanne*. The caption explained that all the dolls had joined the service and that few dolls went to sleep that year as movable eyes use metal (which was needed for war priorities). This is the date for the painted eye *Suzanne* and, of course, *Skippy* was never made as a sleep-eyed doll.

A rotogravure clipping shows "Toys of 1943" and *Suzanne* then appeared to be a sleep-eyed doll.

Black *Skippys* were made but do not show up in any catalogs or advertising. A former Effanbee plant manager has stated that black dolls were made "to special order" in the early days.

It should be noted that Effanbee, as well as some of the catalogs, seemed to have dropped the "Skippy" name for the 1940s military dolls and may not have been paying royalties to the artist at that time. Even so, the doll was so well known that everyone recognized it as *Skippy*. The dolls sold by F.A.O. Schwarz were called *Skippy Sailor* and *Skippy Soldier*.

NOTE: "Skippy" is a copyrighted trademark. Joan Crosby Tibbetts, the daughter of artist Percy L. Crosby, is in charge of current Skippy promotions. The character of Skippy is a humorous juvenile character of comic strip, novel, movie and radio fame. The "Skippy" name is famous as well as the name of a doll. A prize-winning bisque model of Skippy has been recently designed to Mrs. Tibbetts' specifications.

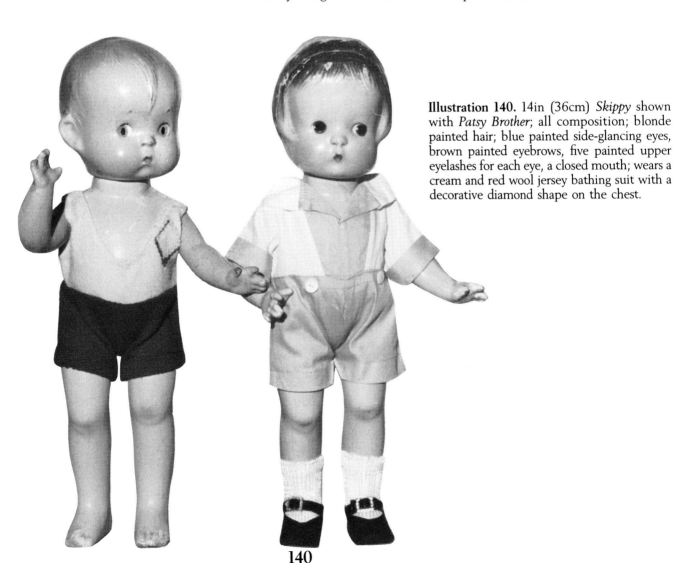

Illustration 140. 14in (36cm) *Skippy* shown with *Patsy Brother*; all composition; blonde painted hair; blue painted side-glancing eyes, brown painted eyebrows, five painted upper eyelashes for each eye, a closed mouth; wears a cream and red wool jersey bathing suit with a decorative diamond shape on the chest.

140

Illustration 143. Advertisement from the June 1931 issue of *Playthings* magazine showing the second or redesigned version of *Skippy*. He no longer has the *Patsy* body. His head is strung on a wooden "button" with a groove near the bottom edge to enable the head to be fastened onto a cloth torso. Elsie R. Baunton designed *Skippy's* clothes.

Illustration 141. 14in (36cm) black *Skippy*; all composition; black painted hair, brown painted side-glancing eyes, black painted eyebrows, five painted upper eyelashes for each eye, a closed mouth; wears a white cotton blouse with a dotted tie, cream trousers, boyish laced oxfords; head is marked: "EFFANBEE//SKIPPY//©// P.L. CROSBY," torso is marked: "EFFanBEE//PATSY//PAT.PEND.// DOLL;" pin on shirt reads: "EFFANBEE//DOLLS//I AM// SKIPPY//TRADE MARK//THE REAL AMERICAN BOY;" 1929. *Joyce Olsen Collection.*

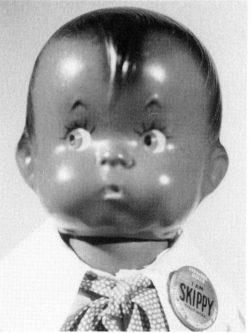

Illustration 142. Close-up of the 14in (36cm) black *Skippy*, seen in *Illustration 141*, showing the detail of the face and the pin. *Joyce Olsen Collection.*

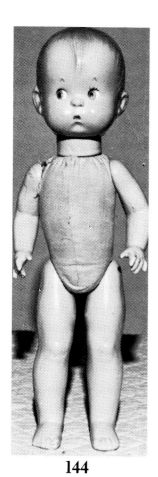

144

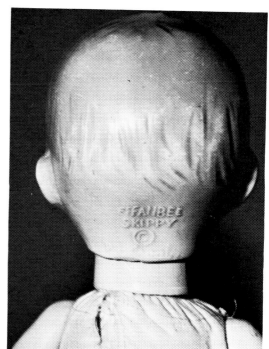

145

Illustration 144. Undressed *Skippy* showing the body construction of the second version with the wooden button with a groove near the bottom edge which enabled it to fit onto a cloth torso.

Illustration 145. Back view of the *Skippy*, seen in *Illustration 144*, showing the neck joint with the wooden button.

146

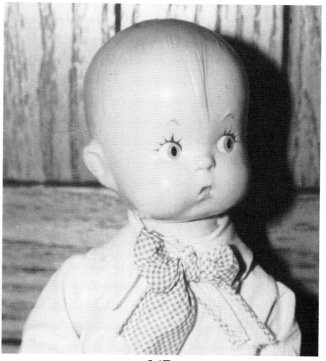

147

Illustration 146. 14in (36cm) *Skippy*; composition head, cloth body, composition arms and legs; painted blonde hair; blue painted side-glancing (to the left) eyes, brown painted eyebrows, five painted upper eyelashes for each eye, a closed mouth; wears a separate white blousey shirt with a blue checked tie, long blue twill trousers sewn to a pantywaist, removable tie oxfords and socks; 1931.

Illustration 147. Close-up of the 14in (36cm) *Skippy*, seen in *Illustration 146*, showing the detail of the costume and the face.

Illustration 148. Real photographs of all-composition 14in (36cm) *Skippy* dolls shown in the Summer 1932 issue of *McCall Decorative Arts & Needlework* magazine modeling actual costumes sewn from McCall pattern number 1994. *Joyce Olsen Collection.*

"SKIPPY" AS COWBOY

149

Illustration 149. Advertisement from the F.A.O. Schwarz 1932 Christmas catalog showing *Skippy* dressed as a cowboy. This appears to be the first type with the *Patsy* body. He wears an elaborate outfit of tan suede leather with nickel studs. One could buy the dressed doll for $4.25 or the suit only for $1.25. A ten-gallon hat cost another $.75.

Illustration 150. 14½in (37cm) *Skippy*; composition head on a wooden button, cloth body, redesigned composition arms and legs; blonde painted hair; blue painted side-glancing eyes, brown painted eyebrows, five painted upper eyelashes for each eye, a closed mouth; wears a white shirt, blue short trousers with button trim, a blue and white checked hat and matching bow tie; marked on the back of the neck: "EFFANBEE// SKIPPY//©//P.L. CROSBY;" pin reads: "EFFanBEE//DOLLS//I AM// SKIPPY//TRADE MARK//THE REAL AMERICAN BOY;" clothing has a satin ink-stamped label on the back reading: "NRA//" and in a heart underneath "EFFanBEE//DURABLE//DOLLS;" circa 1933. The National Industrial Recovery Act was passed by Congress in 1933 and administered by the National Recovery Administration (NRA), following the stock market crash of 1929 and the economic depression. Labels such as these are also found on *Patsy* clothing as well. This version of the cloth-bodied *Skippy* was available in 1931. *Nancy Carlson Collection. Photograph by David Carlson.*

150

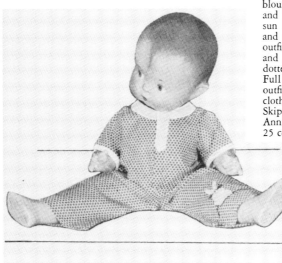

No. 1994. Every youngster wants to have a "boy doll" and even little boys would welcome a doll with such "mannish" attire as this outfit. A "Sunday" suit is shown at center below. It has a white blouse and brown tweed trousers smartly belted. The two-button overcoat and beret match the trousers making a very swagger outfit. The "seamanlike" sailor suit has blue trousers, white middy blouse with star and chevrons on the sleeve, a sailor tie, and "gob" hat. Yellow pique is used for the sun suit and sun hat, and they are trimmed with brown bias binding and the suit appliquéd with a tiny sailboat. The riding outfit has tan breeches, red flannel coat and "jockey" hat, and a white stock at the neck. Peach colored pajamas dotted in white have a cunning appliqué bunny on the leg. Full directions are given in the pattern for making these outfits and also a suit of underwear. Pattern for "Skippy" clothes for Patsy dolls. Sizes, Patsykins 11½ inches, Skippy or Patsy 14 inches, Pasty Joan 16 inches, Patsy Ann 19 inches, and Patsy Lou 22 inches. Pattern, price 25 cents. (30 cents in Canada). Blue embroidery transfer.

1994

Illustration 152. Back view of the 14½ in (37cm) *Skippy*, seen in *Illustrations 150* and *151*, showing the marking on the back of the neck and the placement of the label on the clothing. *Nancy Carlson Collection. Photograph by David Carlson.*

Illustration 153. Close-up of the back of the 14½in (37cm) *Skippy*, seen in *Illustrations 150, 151* and *152*, showing the detail of the label. *Nancy Carlson Collection. Photograph by David Carlson.*

153

152

151

Illustration 151. Close-up of the 14½in (37cm) *Skippy*, seen in *Illustration 150*, showing the detail of the pin as well as the facial features. This pin was not yet created when the prototype doll was introduced in June of 1929. *Nancy Carlson Collection. Photograph by David Carlson.*

154

Illustration 154. Advertisement from Volume 1, Number 3 of *The Patsytown News*, "A Newspaper For Your Doll," in 1934, for *Skippy*. This is a 1929 photograph of the doll. *Marlene Wendt Collection.*

155

156

Illustration 156. Advertisement from a 1936 *American Toy Pictorial* magazine showing a 1931 *Skippy* in a cowboy outfit by Effanbee complete with a ten-gallon hat, a neckerchief, a checked cotton shirt, a vest, chaps and a holster of imitation leather. The holster and chaps were metal studded. *Skippy* was also advertised in 1936 as a Fireman, Sailor, Policeman and Ballplayer as well as a Cowboy. In addition, the June 1936 issue of *Playthings* magazine announced a Scout, Marine and Bellhop.

Illustration 155. 14in (36cm) *Skippy*; composition head on a wooden button, pink muslin body, composition arms and legs with molded white socks and black shoes; brown painted hair; blue painted side-glancing eyes, brown painted eyebrows, five black painted upper eyelashes for each eye, a closed mouth; wears his original baseball uniform with a belt but is missing his cap which was a darker color; 1936. An earlier baseball player was shown in the June 1929 issue of *Toy World* magazine. His striped cotton suit had blousey trousers and he had a matching cap with a bill and special two-tone removable shoes with laces. This was a rare model. The leg mold on the doll shown here and the *Boy Scout* are the same as the leg mold of the later *Skippy Sailor* and *Soldier* from the 1940s. *Rosemary Hanline Collection. Photograph by John Axe.*

157

158

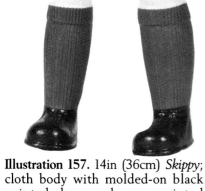

Illustration 157. 14in (36cm) *Skippy*;
cloth body with molded-on black
painted shoes and green painted
socks; brown painted hair; blue
painted side-glancing eyes, brown
painted eyebrows, five painted upper
eyelashes for each eye, a closed mouth;
wears a Boy Scout summer uniform of
khaki color; pin reads: "EFFANBEE//
DOLLS//I AM//SKIPPY//TRADE
MARK//THE REAL AMERICAN
BOY;" 1936. *Photograph by John Axe*.

Illustration 158. Close-up of the 14in
(36cm) *Skippy*, seen in *Illustration
157*. His pin reads: "EFFANBEE//
DOLLS//I AM//SKIPPY//TRADE
MARK//THE REAL AMERICAN
BOY." He dates from 1936. *Photograph by John Axe*.

159

Illustration 159. In the 1940 Effanbee catalog, *Little Lady* and *Skippy* demonstrate
their abilities to hold small metalized toys. The toy card reads: "An//EFFANBEE//
Magic Hand//DOLL//It Picks Up...It Holds...It carries!" The toys on this card are a
United States Flag (which *Skippy* is shown carrying), a parasol (which *Little Lady* is
holding), a broom, a carpet sweeper, a toy dog and a small bouquet which *Little
Lady* is also shown holding. The catalog lists Number 2210, *Sailor Boy*, for $21 per
dozen. The marking on his head, however, is the *Skippy* marking.

160

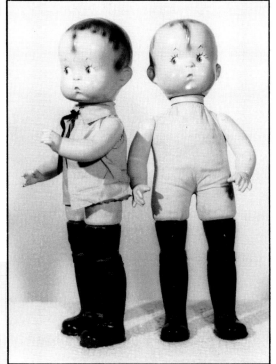

Illustration 160. These two dolls from 1940 show the body and leg construction of the military *Skippy*. Instead of painting the shoes and socks different colors, as was done with the *Boy Scout* and *Baseball Player*, the entire leg was painted brown or black.

Illustration 161. These two 14in (36cm) dolls show the comparison between the two 1940s soldier versions. They both have composition heads on wooden buttons, cloth bodies with composition arms and legs with molded shoes and socks. The doll on the left has magnets in his hands but the doll on the right does not. Except for the hair coloring, the dolls were exactly the same as *Skippy*, including the markings, as the same molds were used. The gold paper heart-shaped tag on the doll on the left reads: "A MAGIC//EFFANBEE//PLAY-MATE//FOR [with a blank space for a name to be written in]//FROM [with a blank space for a name to be written in]//May you and your//dolly have many//happy times together." Doll on the left, *Dorothy Tonkin Collection*.

161

162

Illustration 162. 14in (36cm) *Magic Hand Skippy Soldier* with the magnetic hands; composition head on a wooden button, cloth torso, composition arms and legs; brown painted hair; blue painted side-glancing eyes, brown painted eyebrows, five painted upper eyelashes for each eye, a closed mouth; wears a brown cotton uniform with a shirt, tie, jacket with brass buttons, a garrison cap; gold paper heart-shaped tag reads: "EFFANBEE//Magic Hand//DOLL//IT PICKS UP!//IT HOLDS!//IT CARRIES!;" 1940. This is the same doll shown on the left in *Illustration 161* and the reverse of the tag seen in that illustration is shown here. Note its original box. Evidently royalties were no longer paid to Percy Crosby at this time, yet the same head mold is used with the *Skippy* name. *Dorothy Tonkin Collection*.

Illustration 163. 14in (36cm) *Skippy Aviator*; composition head on a wooden button, cloth torso, composition arms and legs; brown painted hair; blue painted side-glancing eyes, brown painted eyebrows, five painted upper eyelashes for each eye, a closed mouth; wears a ribbed brown cotton suit and helmet with an imitation fur collar plus a belt and pockets, dark brown leatherette goggles; insignia on the chest reads: "KEEP 'EM FLYING;" 1940s.

163

Illustration 164. Close-up of the 14in (36cm) *Skippy Aviator*, seen in *Illustration 163*, showing the detail of the costume and the face.

164

Skippy Soldier

Skippy Sailor

165

Illustration 165. Advertisement from the F.A.O. Schwarz 1941 Christmas catalog featuring dolls with magnetic hands which were new the year before. Shown here are *Skippy Soldier* and *Skippy Sailor*. Dolls with this feature in 1940 were *Sailor, Patsy, Babykin, Patsy Joan, Sugar Baby, Patricia* and *Little Lady*. Dolls added in 1941 were *Military Doll* (*Suzanne*) and *Skippy Soldier*.

1943 Toys

WITH DOLLS REPRESENTING ALL THE SERVICES. THE CLOTH DOLLS ARE $1.39 EACH, THE WAAC $3.96, THE OTHERS $2.49 EACH

167

Illustration 167. These dolls for 1943 reflect the wartime era. *WAC Suzanne*, on the left, cost $3.96. The cloth Red Cross Nurse, next, is not an Effanbee doll but sold for $1.39. The *Skippy Soldiers* and *Sailor* were available for $2.49 each. The 1940 Effanbee catalog lists the *Skippy* with the magnetic hands as simply *Sailor Boy* yet the mold with the *Skippy* marking was still being used. Evidently the company was no longer paying for the use of the name "Skippy."

Illustration 166. 14in (36cm) *Skippy Sailor* with the magnetic hands; composition head on a wooden button, cloth body, composition arms and legs; brown painted hair; blue painted side-glancing eyes, brown painted eyebrows, five painted upper eyelashes for each eye, a closed mouth; wears a two-piece twill navy sailor suit with white braid trim and a cotton neckerchief; marked on the back of the head: "SKIPPY//©// P.L. CROSBY." He holds one of the miniature toys, a toy mop to scrub the decks of his ship. *Margaret Ashbrook Collection.*

166

Chapter Five

Patsy Ann,

Big Sister to *Patsy,* and Her Variants

"'PATSY ANN' breaks a record!" was the very first headline in the trade magazines on the second *Patsy* version in the family series appearing in an advertisement in the June 29, 1929, issue of *Toys and Novelties* magazine. The copy explained: "It is amazing how quickly this new Effanbee doll has captured popular fancy with her tantalizing demureness. She is wistful one minute and impish the next. But whatever Patsy Ann's mood, she is as irresistible as the first Spring day — and just as refreshing."

Full-page advertisements would run in the trade magazines for June, July, August and September in 1929. The doll wore a gold paper heart-shaped tag on the arm which read: "This is//PATSY-ANN//TRADE MARK PAT. PEND.//The Lovable Imp//with tiltable head//and movable limb//An//EFFanBEE//DURABLE//DOLL."

Illustration 168. Advertisement for *Patsy Ann* in the June 1929 issue of *Toys and Novelties.* There were no gold metal heart-shaped bracelet tags at this time, only the gold paper heart-shaped tag with the black printing announcing: "This is//PATSY-ANN// TRADE MARK PAT. PEND.//The Lovable Imp//with tiltable head//and movable limb//AN//EFFanBEE//DU-RABLE//DOLL."

168

TOYS AND NOVELTIES—June, 1929   7

"PATSY ANN"
breaks a record!

It is amazing how quickly this new Effanbee doll has captured popular fancy with her tantalizing demureness. She is wistful one minute and impish the next. But whatever Patsy Ann's mood, she is as irresistible as the first Spring day— and just as refreshing.

Salesrooms:
45 East 17th St.
New York

General Office:
45 Greene St.
New York

FLEISCHAKER & BAUM
Manufacturers of Effanbee Dolls

"OF COURSE IT'S AN EFFANBEE DOLL...."

WHEN ANSWERING ADVERTISEMENTS, PLEASE MENTION TOYS AND NOVELTIES

At her debut, *Patsy Ann* is shown wearing a flowered piqué coat and hat with a felt brim and felt trim on the collar, cuffs and pocket of the coat. Half-page advertisements in the *American Weekly* comic section of the Sunday newspaper for December 1929 showed the same doll in color. The outfit was said to come in tangerine and blue or maize and green. This model cost $7.50 but the doll was available in other styles for $5.00.

The news articles in *Toys and Novelties* magazine for December 1930 showed *Patsy Ann* in a party dress with a high yoke and full skirt with two ruffles at the hem. Ribbon rosettes with streamers trimmed the yoke. She was to be featured in the Effanbee advertising campaign to be launched in the *American Weekly* newspapers.

The same official portrait was used in the December 1930 issue of *Junior Home*, a children's magazine, along with a featured photograph of the baby doll *Lovums*. The description of *Patsy Ann* reads: "Wonderful Patsy Ann. Here is Patsy Ann — all ready for Christmas with a dainty new organdy dress. She is so impish and demure — such a grand playmate for every little girl. And be sure you get the original Patsy Ann with the durable all-composition body."

This same photograph was used a year later in the November 1931 *Junior Home* magazine. The tag is a paper one as there were no metal bracelet tags at this time. The copy read:

"Patsy and her brothers and sisters are such wonderful playmates for you. You can dress, dance and play with them and just think — all their clothes can be washed. The best thing about these wonder dolls is that they will last for years. That's because they are Effanbee Durable Dolls, made by the special Effanbee process.

Illustration 169. Artwork done by Effanbee to claim a patent for *Patsy Ann* in an effort to discourage competitors and encourage purchasers to acquire the genuine item. The marking reads: "EFFanBEE//PATSY ANN//©//PAT.# 1283558." Actually, this patent had been issued about five years earlier and did not refer to the neck joint, yet this sketch would be used on the certificate of membership in the *Patsy* Doll Club and various issues of *The Patsytown News*.

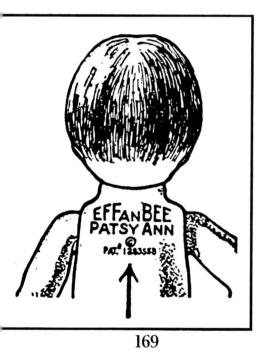

169

Illustration 170. 19in (48cm) *Patsy Ann*; all composition; painted hair with a ribbon rosette bandeau around her hair; blue tin sleep eyes, one-stroke eyebrows, real hair eyelashes; wears original floral organdy dress with a ribbon rosette at the waist, a combination undergarment with lace at the legs and a separate ruffled petticoat; gold paper heart-shaped tag reads: "This is//PATSY-ANN//TRADE MARK PAT. PEND.//The Lovable Imp//with tiltable head// and movable limb//AN//EFFanBEE//DURABLE// DOLL." *Nancy Carlson Collection. Photograph by David Carlson.*

170

"You can tell Effanbee Dolls by their golden heart necklace or emblem. There's a big family of them, ranging in price from $1 to $25. At department and toy stores."

The golden heart-shaped necklace came on some baby and mama dolls. The emblem is the gold paper heart-shaped tag.

The November 1930 issue of *Good Housekeeping* magazine showed *Patsy Ann* in a party dress with continuous ruffles on the skirt bottom. One could buy a dressed doll by mail for $4.95 in a pink, blue, maize or green organdy frock. Pattern number N-21 was also available for $.35 and included a romper, a zip-on aviator suit and helmet, a school dress, a beach pajama set, undies and a swimsuit. We have been unable to locate any of the patterns offered by this magazine, however.

By the time the colored newspaper illustration appeared on November 29, 1931, the *Patsy Ann* party dress was a somewhat different model of pink with lace at the neck edge and armholes, shirring at the neck in blue and two ruffles at the hem with the top ruffle not going across the front. Ribbons trimmed the front ruffle edge.

She was said to come in plain colors or flowered for $5.00 or $5.50 west of the Mississippi. Here *Patsy* is mentioned as being 14in (36cm) tall.

By March 1932, the full-page Fleischaker & Baum advertisement in *Playthings* magazine featured illustrations for three dolls — *Patsy Ann*, *Patsy* and *Skippy*. An artist has sketched them all on roller skates. A little poetic license is taken as the knees are bent a bit more than would have been possible on the real doll. By this time, *Patsy Ann*, *Patsy Joan*, *Patsy*, *Patsy Lou*, *Patsykins*, *Skippy*, *Patsyette* and *Lamkin* have all been created. What fun it must have been for little girls to get them all new and beautiful, one by one.

Illustration 172. 19in (48cm) *Patsy Ann*, seen in *Illustrations 170* and *171*, shown in her original tailored coat and hat which could possibly have been made by the F.A.O. Schwarz firm. *Nancy Carlson Collection. Photograph by David Carlson.*

172

Illustration 173. Close-up of the original gold paper heart-shaped tag worn by the 19in (48cm) *Patsy Ann*, seen in *Illustrations 170, 171* and *172*. The gold metal heart-shaped bracelet tag was not available until 1932. This doll is circa 1930. *Nancy Carlson Collection. Photograph by David Carlson.*

Illustration 171. 19in (48cm) *Patsy Ann*, seen in *Illustration 170*, shown in her ruffled petticoat and undergarments. *Nancy Carlson Collection. Photograph by David Carlson.*

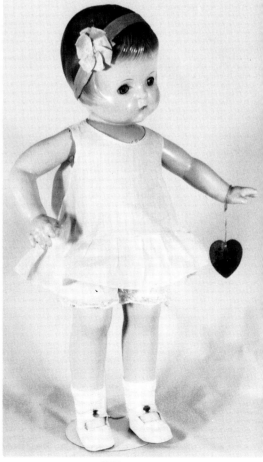

173

171

From an original folio in our collection titled "NEW EFFANBEE CREATIONS," featuring *Tousle Head* (with a *Lovums* head) in a lamb skin wig, *Sugar Baby* and *Lovums* on one side and *Patsykin*, *Patsy Ann* and *Patsy* on the reverse, we gain the following information:

"This is Patsy Ann in a play mood. Sometimes she is impish and sometimes demure. Patsy Ann has such wonderful expressive eyes, with real long eyelashes. You cannot help adoring such a dear little sister. Of course you must see her exciting new roller skates that come already attached to her shoes. Just think what fun it will be to take Patsy Ann roller skating. She is 19 inches tall."

The *Patsys'* Fingernail Fiasco

Fleischaker & Baum not only manufactured high-grade satin-smooth composition dolls which were beautifully costumed, but the firm worked very hard to create a climate of excitement and wonder for the dolls.

One of these big campaigns to create something entirely different in a doll must have brought about problems beyond measure, the details of which are now lost in the mist of time.

It was 1936 when the big advertising campaign in *Toys and Novelties* magazine was announced:

"Patsy"
"New In Sophistication!"
"Effanbee beauty parlor has performed a real miracle in make-up that you shouldn't miss, an improvement that will delight all 'Patsy' fans. This new secret of Patsy's poise and sophistication will be a <u>permanent</u> part of her make up. See her at the Effanbee showroom."

In August of 1936, *Playthings* magazine advertised *Dy-Dee Baby*, the *Patsy* family, the movie *Anne Shirley* doll and *Sugar Baby*. The copy read: "The Patsy Family, whimsical, lovable, profitable! This year all Patsys have FINGERNAILS — a big talking point."

175

Illustration 175. 19in (48cm) *Patsy Ann*; all composition; brown painted hair; blue-gray metal sleep eyes, brown painted eyebrows, a closed mouth; wears a multi-colored balloon motif dress, similar to the one shown on the doll in the advertisement in *Illustration 174*, with a white cotton collar embroidered in red with a matching ribbon bow; 1929. This is apparently an early Effanbee style of dress which evidently was later decided to be too long in length. Future factory designs were usually well above the knees. Some earlier dolls had composition legs to just above the knees and then cloth upper legs, thus necessitating this longer style.

4239—Patsy Ann's personality matches her perky little hairbow. She is 19½ inches tall, and made of unusually sturdy composition, with eyes that open and close, and jointed arms and legs. **$4.95.**

174

Illustration 174. Advertisement from the Marshall Field & Co. 1929 Christmas catalog for an all-composition 19½in (48cm) *Patsy Ann*. She wears a multi-colored cotton dress with an embroidered collar and ribbon trim. The angle of the camera makes the dress appear to be even longer than it actually was. She was available for $4.95.

In Effanbee's *The Patsytown News*, Volume 3 for fall 1936, page three carried the following headline: "Now Patsy Has Beautiful Fingernails!" The sub-heading declared: "Effanbee Beauty Shop Makes Patsy's Hand Look Just Like Real Little Girls." The story continued:

"Patsy is so happy! And so proud of her new, really truly finger nails that she and all her older sisters now have! And no wonder! For her new finger nails look exactly like real human nails — and they're all beautifully polished too."

"It all happened when Patsy and her bigger sisters stopped in at the Effanbee Beauty Shop one day to have their beautiful hair fixed. After their hair had been combed out nice and neat, and all the curls carefully arranged, the manager of the Effanbee Beauty Shop said, 'My, but you're certainly a nice-looking group of young girls. What can I do to make you prettier. I know! Let me do your finger nails.'

"'Oh, that would be nice!' chorused Patsy and her sisters. And so the Effanbee Beauty Shop manager made some beautiful, real-life finger nails for their hands, put them on, and polished them to a beautiful, lustrous sheen.

"'Oh, oh, oh!' said Patsy and her sisters. 'These are lovely!' The Patsys certainly did feel proud and happy!

"'Now you look sweeter than ever,' the Beauty Shop Manager said. 'And from now on I'm going to put real finger nails on all Patsys and their older sisters before they leave the great big Effanbee Factory.'

"You can see Patsy and her larger sisters with their new finger nails when you visit the toy department at the store. The new finger nails are made separately, and permanently attached so that they will never come off. And they make Patsy's hand look just like a real little girl's hand!"

A full-length photograph of *Patsy Ann* was shown with a longer and fuller wig than was used earlier, seemingly marcelled with just the ends

176

177

Illustration 177. Close-up of the 19in (48cm) *Twin Brother* to *Patsy Ann*, seen in *Illustration 176*. Ursula Mertz Collection. Photograph by Otto Mertz.

Illustration 176. 19in (48cm) *Twin Brother* to *Patsy Ann* modeling a brown velvet party outfit with a white cotton shirt. He is all original and wears the Effanbee pin with the heart on it. There are two pearl buttons on the side of each pants leg. He is from circa 1930. *Ursula Mertz Collection. Photograph by Otto Mertz.*

curled up. Her head is tilted forward as though contemplating her fingernails. She wears the gold paper heart-shaped tag on one arm and the gold metal heart-shaped bracelet tag on the other. The caption under the photograph states: "Patsy Ann is so proud of her new, realistic finger nails that she just can't stop admiring them. And who can blame her! They look just like the real finger nails on her little mother's hand." A close-up in an oval is shown of the hand where you can see white cuticles and very dark fingernails. Whether they were actually painted this deep red is not certain as the author has yet to see a mint all-original doll.

These examples had ovals of clear celluloid glued into a little recess in the finger tips. They are very rare. We saw one for sale many years ago with more of the nails missing than not. We have seen a second doll recently which happened to be a *Patricia* version with some nails missing.

Of all the hundreds of Effanbee *Patsys* we have observed, no other fingernailed *Patsys* have surfaced despite the extensive advertising. One or two examples have been reported in correspondence.

It must have been that only the very first group of the planned fingernailed *Patsys* went on the market before they were recalled or discontinued as they would not otherwise be so scarce. Some of the dolls' hands which followed had recessed molded areas indicating the fingernail which was either left natural or tinted a rosy pink. This seems a much more appropriate solution for a young child's doll. However, from a collector's point of view, if you have a *Patsy/Patricia* with added celluloid fingernails intact, you have a rare collector's item indeed!

Illustration 178. 19in (48cm) *Twin Brother* to *Patsy Ann*; all composition; painted hair; sleep eyes, painted eyebrows, a closed mouth; wears an all-original green and white cotton suit with pearl button trim on the shirt and pants legs, belt stitched on the sides. *Pat Brill Collection.*

178

Illustration 179. Side view of the 19in (48cm) *Twin Brother* to *Patsy Ann*, seen in *Illustration 178. Pat Brill Collection.*

Illustration 180. Advertisement from the November 1931 issue of *Junior Home* magazine for *Patsy* and her brothers and sisters. This contemporary Effanbee photograph was also used in the same magazine in 1930. No mention was made of the *Patsy* Club in 1930.

179

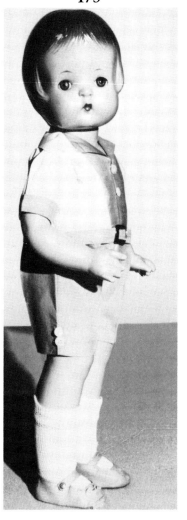

180

The Gay Patsy Family

Patsy and her brothers and sisters are such wonderful playmates for you. You can dress, dance and play with them and just think—all their clothes can be washed. The best thing about these wonder dolls is that they will last for years. That's because they are Effanbee Durable Dolls, made by the special Effanbee process.

You can tell Effanbee Dolls by their golden heart necklace or emblem. There's a big family of them, ranging in price from $1 to $25. At department and toy stores.

Mail coupon for Patsy Club Membership Button and Certificate for your doll. You'll also get a copy of the new magazine.

EFFANBEE DOLLS

Patsy Effanbee, % Fleischaker & Baum, Dept. G-12, 45 Greene St., New York City.
Send me Patsy Club Membership Button and Certificate, also the new Club Magazine. I enclose 2c postage.

Name ....
Street ....
City.. State..............

TRUNK TROUSSEAU

Adorable trunk trousseau. The trunk is green, with brass corners and trim and lock. It has the cutest wooden hangers and three drawers for the underwear and things. The doll—you may have the trousseau for three different ones—fits nicely into the side of the trunk.

No. A-78—Trunk 22" with the 19" dressed **Patsy Ann** Doll, including two extra dresses with underwear, beach pajamas, silk pajamas, bathrobe, coat and hat, sweater and hat, shoes, socks and roller skates $25.00

181

Illustration 181. 19in (48cm) *Patsy Ann* was featured by F.A.O. Schwarz in its 1931 Christmas catalog, and also in 1932, in a trunk trousseau which was also available for *Patsy Joan* and *Patsy.* The green trunk had brass corners, trim and lock, wooden hangers and three drawers for underwear and other small items. The trunk was 22in (56cm) tall so the doll could fit inside nicely. The clothing included two extra dresses, underwear, beach pajamas, silk pajamas, a bathrobe, a coat and hat, a sweater and hat, shoes, socks and roller skates. The cost was $25.

184

183

182

Illustration 182. 19in (48cm) *Patsy Ann* dolls; all composition. The doll on the left has reddish painted hair; brown sleep eyes, a closed mouth and wears her original faded blue cotton batiste dress with a two-tone blue ruffle at the bottom and matching collar and cuffs. The doll on the right is the highly sought-after black version with black painted hair; brown metal sleep eyes and wears her original dress of white cotton with a floral design of green leaves and yellow blossoms and a deep batiste collar edged in lace. Doll on the right, *Betty Lucas Collection.*

Illustration 183. 19in (48cm) black *Patsy Ann*, seen in *Illustration 182*, models a specialty shop coat of light brown felt trimmed in darker brown with pink and blue felt flowerets hand-stitched onto the coat and beret. *Betty Lucas Collection.*

Illustration 184. Close-up of the 19in (48cm) black *Patsy Ann*, seen in *Illustrations 182* and *183*, showing the detail of the trim on the clothing as well as the painting of the face. Her mouth is a pink-rose shade and her eyebrows are black. *Betty Lucas Collection.*

Illustration 185. Advertisement from the November 1931 *Good Housekeeping* magazine introducing *Patsy Ann*. She came fully dressed from Effanbee in an organdy dress in pink, blue, maize or green. Her cost was $4.95. She is surrounded by sketches of garments which could be made from pattern number N-21 which included the aviator cap and suit with a zipper. Later these outfits for children would come to be known as snowsuits.

185

187

Illustration 187. 19in (48cm) *Patsy Ann*; all composition; brown mohair wig; models cotton beach pajamas in pink, yellow, lavender and green stripes with plain apple green trim, a sun hat with a striped brim which has eight rows of stitching on the scalloped brim. This is possibly a creation from the F.A.O. Schwarz studios.

186

Illustration 186. Original advertisement from the March 1932 issue of *Playthings* magazine for the *Patsy* family and *Skippy*. Note that *Patsy Ann*, *Patsykins*, *Patsyette*, *Patsy Joan*, *Patsy Lou* and *Lamkin* are also mentioned.

HURRY, GIRLS!

DECEMBER 14, 1930.

The Doll Girl and Her Wonder Babies Will Only Be
Here a Few Days Longer — Her Dollies Are Saying:

"I WANT A HOME"

FREE

FREE

"Patsy Ann"

It's such fun to play with rosy-cheeked "Patsy Ann" pictured here. She stands 19 inches tall and is asking for some little girl to be her "Mama."

"Tickletoes"

This pretty doll has rubber arms and legs and measures 18 inches from her little toes to her dainty bonnet. She has three voices, one in each leg and one in her body.

"Lovums"

This new baby was called "Lovums" because she is so lovable. Who could help loving such a dear little sister? Be sure to see her when you visit the P.-I. Doll Girl.

"Marilee"

"Marilee" is 20 inches tall and has beautiful brown curls and eyelashes. You'll love her dainty dresses and the way she calls "Mama."

*Be Your Own
Santa Claus*

*Get Started
Now
Win a Doll*

Illustration 188. Original advertisement from the December 14, 1930, *Seattle Post-Intelligencer* for a 19in (48cm) *Patsy Ann* which was available from the newspaper for new subscriptions. The Effanbee Doll company had always sold some dolls via newspaper or magazine subscription drives from the 1920s on. Newspapers could order the dolls wholesale, probably in the costume of the previous season, and offer them to the public for subscriptions obtained. The material of *Patsy Ann's* dress, shown here, is a cotton sateen and was also used on a *Rosemary* mama doll in shades of gold and brown. *Lovums* and *Marilee*, mentioned here, were also by Effanbee while *Tickletoes* was manufactured by the Ideal Novelty and Toy Company.

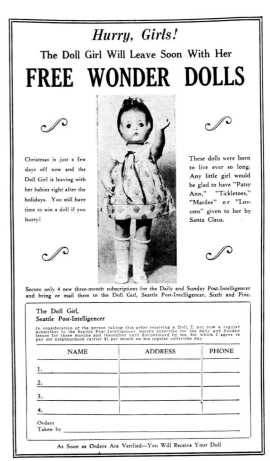

Hurry, Girls!
The Doll Girl Will Leave Soon With Her

FREE WONDER DOLLS

Christmas is just a few days off now and the Doll Girl is leaving with her babies right after the holidays. You still have time to win a doll if you hurry!

These dolls were born to live ever so long. Any little girl would be glad to have "Patsy Ann," "Tickletoes," "Marilee" or "Lovums" given to her by Santa Claus.

Secure only 4 new three-month subscriptions for the Daily and Sunday Post-Intelligencer and bring or mail them to the Doll Girl, Seattle Post-Intelligencer, Sixth and Pine.

The Doll Girl,
Seattle Post-Intelligencer

In consideration of the person taking this order receiving a Doll, I, not now a regular subscriber to the Seattle Post-Intelligencer, hereby subscribe for the daily and Sunday issues for three months and thereafter until discontinued by me, for which I agree to pay my neighborhood carrier $1 per month on his regular collection day.

NAME	ADDRESS	PHONE
1.		
2.		
3.		
4.		

Orders
Taken by

As Soon as Orders Are Verified—You Will Receive Your Doll

189

Illustration 189. A later original advertisement for a 19in (48cm) *Patsy Ann* from the December 21, 1930, *Seattle Post-Intelligencer* available for new subscriptions.

Illustration 190. Original advertisement for a 19in (48cm) *Patsy Ann* from the November 28, 1932, *Seattle Post-Intelligencer* available for new subscriptions. Note that she is in a different outfit than those shown in *Illustrations 188* and *189* and her dress is said to be of blue or pink silk.

Make Some Little Girl Happy This Christmas With a

"Patsy Ann" Doll

Given FREE by the POST-INTELLIGENCER

NOVEMBER 28, 1932.

RULES

1—To win a doll there must be four new subscriptions in all, for at least three months each, daily and Sunday.

2—Subscription must be signed by the subscriber, not by the contestant.

3—All orders must be from new subscribers, not those already receiving the Post-Intelligencer. Stopping one paper and starting another, changing the name from one member of the family to another at the same address, or changing the paper from one address to another, do NOT make NEW subscriptions out of OLD ones.

4—Mail or bring in EACH ORDER as you get it. Don't wait to send them all in at once, as each subscriber will be anxious to receive his paper.

5—Subscription orders are subject to verification by the Seattle Post-Intelligencer.

6—Collect no money unless out of Seattle, to be sent by mail. Three dollars must accompany each mail subscription.

HERE'S "PATSY ANN"!

Rosy-cheeked "Patsy Ann" stands nineteen inches high, and will delight the heart of any girl. She sells for $5 in any of the stores, and you may have her in either blue or pink silk dress!

190

Illustration 191. Another original advertisement for a 19in (48cm) *Patsy Ann* from the November 24, 1932, *Seattle Post-Intelligencer* available for new subscriptions. She still comes in a blue or pink silk dress.

Illustration 192. Another original advertisement for a 19in (48cm) *Patsy Ann* from the November 30, 1932, *Seattle Post-Intelligencer* available in a blue or pink silk dress for new subscriptions.

HERE'S "PATSY ANN"!

Rosy - cheeked "Patsy Ann" stands nineteen inches high, and will delight the heart of any girl. She sells for $5 in any of the stores, and you may have her in either blue or pink silk dress!

Make Some Little Girl Happy This Christmas!

192

Make This A Happy Christmas
For Some Little Girl - - -

With A "Patsy Ann" Doll

〉 Given
〉 Free of Cost
〉 by the
〉 Seattle
〉 Post-Intelligencer

HERE'S HOW TO GET HER: Have four of your friends who are NOT subscribers to the Post-Intelligencer sign the blanks, agreeing to take the Daily and Sunday paper for three months each. Send in the orders as you get them, and as soon as they are verified, "Patsy Ann" is yours. You only collect on mail subscriptions.

HERE'S "PATSY ANN"!

19 inches high, blue or pink silk dress, and sells for $5 in the stores!

Send or bring this order to the Post-Intelligencer office as soon as it is signed

TO SUBSCRIBER: PAY NO MONEY TO SOLICITOR

Date.........................1933.

In consideration of the person taking this order receiving a "Patsy Ann"-doll, I hereby subscribe for the Daily and Sunday issues of the Seattle Post-Intelligencer for three months and thereafter until discontinued by me, for which I agree to pay my neighborhood carrier $1.00 per month on his regular collection day. I am NOT now a subscriber.

NAME ....
ADDRESS ....
APT. NO. .... PHONE................
ORDER SECURED BY.........................
ADDRESS ....

FOUR

Coupons in all are required. Use the one opposite and cut more from tomorrow's paper.

CALL, PHONE OR WRITE

CIRCULATION DEPARTMENT

MAin 2000

Seattle Post-Intelligencer

SIXTH AND PINE

191

Illustration 193. Yet another original advertisement for a 19in (48cm) *Patsy Ann* from the December 10, 1932, *Seattle Post-Intelligencer* available for new subscriptions, still in her pink or blue silk dress.

Here's all you have to do to get a doll: Get 4 new subscriptions to the Post-Intelligencer, for at least 3 months each, daily and Sunday.

Subscription must be signed by the subscriber, not by the contestant.

All orders must be from new subscribers, not those already receiving the Post-Intelligencer. Stopping one paper and starting another, changing the name from one member of the family to another at the same address, or changing the paper from one address to another, do NOT make NEW subscriptions out of OLD ones.

Mail or bring in EACH ORDER as you get it. Don't wait to send them all in at once, as each subscriber will be anxious to receive his paper.

Subscription orders are subject to verification by the Seattle Post-Intelligencer.

Collect no money unless out of Seattle, to be sent by mail. Three dollars must accompany each mail subscription.

Subscription Blank

TO SUBSCRIBER: PAY NO MONEY TO SOLICITOR. Send or mail this order to the Post-Intelligencer as soon as it is signed.

Date ....

In consideration of the person taking this order receiving a "Patsy Ann" Doll, I hereby subscribe for the daily and Sunday issues of the Seattle Post-Intelligencer for three months and thereafter until discontinued by me, for which I agree to pay my neighborhood carrier $1 per month on his regular collection day. I am NOT now a subscriber.

1 ....
(Name)

Address ....

Apt......... Phone..............
Order Secured

By ....

This Beautiful 'Patsy Ann' DOLL

Post-Intelligencer

6th and Pine . . . MAin 2000

193

Illustration 195. Close-up of the 19in (48cm) *Patsy Ann*, seen in *Illustration 194*, showing the detail of the face as well as the smocking and the trim on the dress. *Glorya Woods Collection. Photograph by Glorya Woods.*

Illustration 196. Original advertisement from the January 1932 issue of *Playthings* magazine referred to the "Dog Days" of business from the Depression era. Many who yearned for *Patsy* dolls could not afford to buy them. Featured together are *Patsy Ann* and her *Twin Brother* in rare outfits.

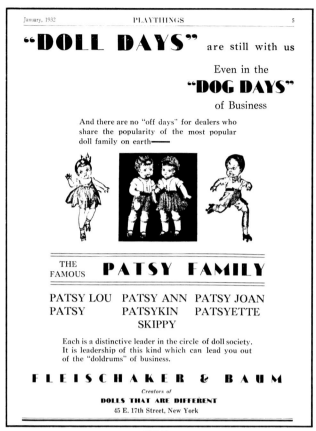

195

194

196

Illustration 194. 19in (48cm) *Patsy Ann*; all composition; painted reddish hair with a pink hair bow; green sleep eyes, painted eyebrows, a closed mouth; wears a pale pink silk dress with a row of pink smocking followed by a row of green smocking at the front neck, double-faced pink and green silk ribbon rosette and streamers trim the neckline. Her heart-shaped bracelet has been added. She is circa 1931. *Glorya Woods Collection. Photograph by Glorya Woods.*

197

Illustration 197. Original advertisement from the 1932 Montgomery Ward catalog showing *Skippy, Patsyette, Patsykins, Patsy* and *Patsy Ann* which were all available. All the dolls in this group had painted eyes except for *Patsy Ann*. The small nude doll was shown to indicate the dolls were entirely composition and did not have stuffed bodies.

Illustration 198. 19in (48cm) *Patsy Ann*; all composition; reddish-brown painted hair; green sleep eyes, painted brown eyebrows, real hair upper eyelashes, a closed mouth; wears a dress of dotted flocked (not woven) material of white and green with hand-embroidered motifs on the white lace-trimmed collar. The dress is the same pattern as one illustrated in a 1932 Sears, Roebuck and Co. catalog. Dress, *Nancy Carlson Collection.*

Illustration 199. 19in (48cm) *Patsy Ann*; all composition; painted hair; metal sleep eyes, painted eyebrows, painted and real hair upper eyelashes, painted lower eyelashes, a closed rosebud mouth; wears original red cotton sheer dress with a white piqué inset yoke which has red cross-stitches on it, a Peter Pan collar, puff sleeves, a deep hem on a full skirt; dress has a satin printed label with a heart reading: "EFFANBEE//DURABLE// DOLLS;" wears a gold metal heart-shaped bracelet tag reading: "EFFANBEE//PATSY//ANN." The floral headband has been added. *Inge Simms Collection.*

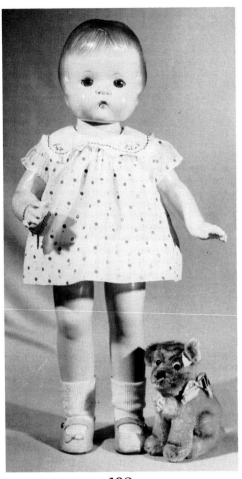

198

199

Illustration 200. Close-up of the 19in (48cm) *Patsy Ann*, seen in *Illustration 199*, showing the detail of the dress and the face. *Inge Simms Collection.*

200

Illustration 201. Close-up of the 19in (48cm) *Patsy Ann*, seen in *Illustrations 199* and *200*, showing the gold metal heart-shaped bracelet tag she is wearing. These metal tags were not made until 1932. *Inge Simms Collection.*

Illustration 202. Back view of the 19in (48cm) *Patsy Ann*, seen in *Illustrations 199, 200* and *201*, showing the back of the dress and the placement of the label on the dress. *Inge Simms Collection.*

202

201

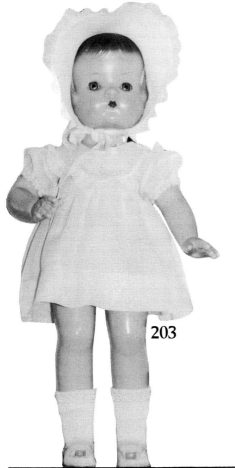

203

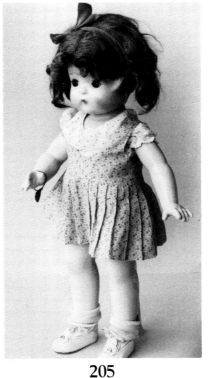

205

Illustration 205. 19in (48cm) *Patsy Ann;* all composition; brown mohair wig; brown sleep eyes, painted eyebrows, real hair upper eyelashes, a closed mouth; wears a combination blouse/romper of white cotton with red polka dots, a cotton jumper of yellow with red flowers, white socks with yellow stripes, white leather tie-on shoes which are usually found on the larger mama dolls. *Joan Eesley Collection. Photograph by Joan Eesley.*

Illustration 206. The 1933 Christmas catalog for Marshall Field & Co. featured a 19in (48cm) *Patsy Ann* in a pink organdy dress with touches of blue embroidery and a pink bonnet tied with blue ribbon, pink shoes and white socks with pink bands at the tops, all for $5.95.

Patsy Dolls Now Have Wigs!

1933

Lovely curling locks or straight bobs of mohair; blonde, brunette or auburn. These lovable little imps tilt their heads and move their arms and legs. They all have stylish new Dresses. (Felt Coats and Hats at slight additional prices!)

Patsy Ann   Patsy Joan   Patsy   Patsykins   Patsyette

204

Illustration 203. 19in (48cm) *Patsy Ann;* all composition; red-brown painted hair; green glassene sleep eyes, painted eyebrows, a closed mouth; wears a dress of yellow organdy with a deep ruffled collar trimmed with green embroidered motifs, matching brimmed and ruffled bonnet, a combination suit with a slip; dress is labeled: "Effanbee." *Bothwell/Chapman Collection. Photograph by owner.*

Illustration 204. Original advertisement from an unknown newspaper in 1933 which mentions only mohair wigs for the *Patsy* dolls although many dolls also had human hair wigs, but this may have been later. *Patsyette* was the only size which came with a straight bobbed wig. The dolls at this time had the small gold metal heart-shaped bracelet tags as well as the gold paper heart-shaped tags.

Patsy Ann, 4204, is the name of the pretty doll in the center—the joy of any little girl. She has real lashes and eyes that close, and a lustrous, curly mohair wig. Her body and head are composition, and she wears a dainty organdy dress and bonnet. 19″ tall. $5.95.

206

207

Illustration 208. 19in (48cm) *Patsy Ann* with a wig, modeling the 1934 version of her silk frock and matching bonnet. She now comes with the gold metal heart-shaped bracelet tag as well as the gold paper heart-shaped tag. Her dress has a short yoke, a deep ruffled collar with ribbon streamer trim and decorative tucks above the hem. This is from *The Patsytown News*, Volume 1, Number 3, page 4, from 1934.

Patsy Ann with her silk frock and personality wig.

208

Illustration 207. 19in (48cm) *Patsy Ann* modeling a costume designed for the 1933 wigged-version of the doll. A white blouse with blue polka dots is attached to the panties which match the jumper. The small patterned print is on a blue background. What is left of a sewn-in Effanbee label is in the back. The shoes have been replaced. *Martha Sweeney Collection. Photograph by Martha Sweeney.*

Illustration 209. 19in (48cm) *Patsy Ann* with a wig, wearing a white fur coat and matching tam-o'-shanter. There was a size made for every *Patsy* doll. Storm rubbers and galoshes were available as well. For warmer weather, *Patsy Ann* had a tailored velvet coat with a hat to match which came in red, green or blue. This is from *The Patsytown News*, Volume 1, Number 4, from 1934.

LET THE WINTER WINDS BLOW

Miss Patsy Ann is Snug and Warm in Her New Fur Coat

Cold winter winds can't bother Patsy Ann now—all snug and warm in her stylish new white fur coat, with fashionable fur tam o'shanter to match. She certainly is a handsome little girl, all dressed up for winter's worst weather. And she's so proud! Her coat fits perfectly, and is made from fine, long-wearing fur. There's a size for every Patsy Doll—and every Patsy should have one this winter.

(Oh!—we almost forgot to tell you about Patsy's pretty, new storm rubbers and golashes which keep her feet warm and dry in snowy and rainy weather.)

And for warmer weather, Patsy has a beautifully tailored, up-to-date velvet coat with a pretty hat to match, in the latest shades of red, green or blue. See them at your department store.

Patsy Ann in her Stylish Fur Coat and Hat

209

RIGHT: **Color Illustration 64.** Undressed rare black World War II *Skippy Sailor. Lucia Kirsch Collection.*

BELOW: **Color Illustration 65.** All-original World War II *Skippy Sailor* with his original box. *Ursula Mertz Collection. Photograph by Otto Mertz.*

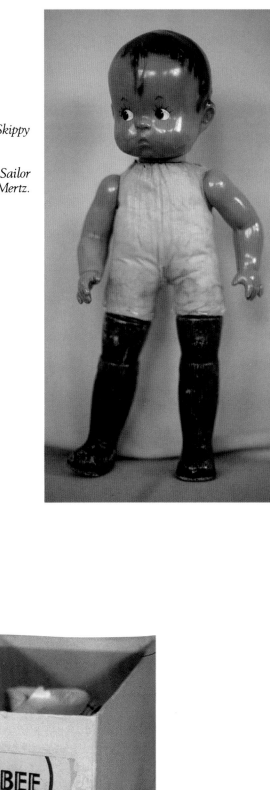

ABOVE: Color Illustration 66. Comparative view of four *Patsykins*, left to right: a *Patsykins* with molded hair and painted eyes wearing a blue dotted homemade dress; a *Patsykins* with a mohair wig and painted eyes wearing an outfit made from a McCall pattern; a *Patsykins* with molded hair and painted eyes in her original dotted swiss dress by Effanbee; a *Patsykins* with painted hair and metal sleep eyes wearing a teddy made from a McCall pattern.

RIGHT: Color Illustration 67. Comparative view of several *Patsykins* variants, left to right: the movie *Anne Shirley*, a rare black version in her original Effanbee party dress and an all-original version with tin sleep eyes wearing a party dress. *Inge Simms Collection.*

Color Illustration 68. All-original black *Patsykins* with pigtails and wearing her original Effanbee clothing. *Inge Simms Collection.*

OPPOSITE PAGE: Color Illustration 69. All-original *Patsykins* wearing an organdy party dress and bonnet. *Inge Simms Collection.*

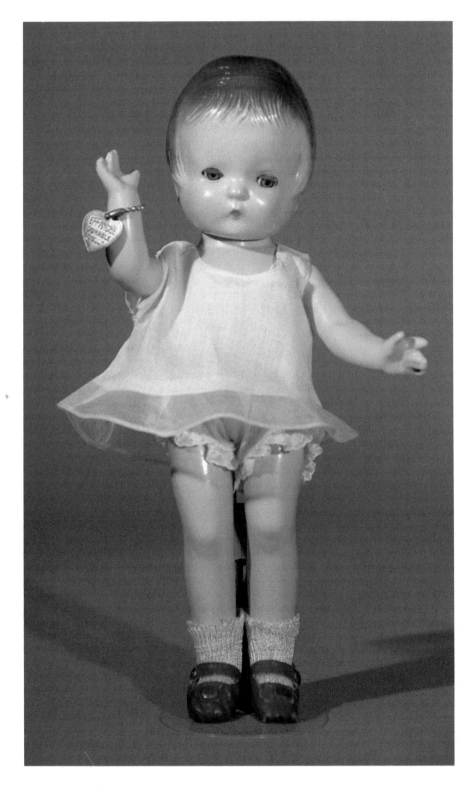

ABOVE: Color Illustration 70. Side view of the all-original *Patsykins*, seen in *Color Illustration 69. Inge Simms Collection.*

LEFT: Color Illustration 71. All-original *Patsykins*, seen in *Color Illustrations 69* and *70*, wearing her pink teddy and separate slip by Effanbee. *Inge Simms Collection.*

LEFT: Color Illustration 72. All-original *Patsykins* wearing a pink batiste ensemble with a white collar and bonnet brim, by Effanbee. *Jackie Rovick Collection.*

BELOW: Color Illustration 73. *Patsykins* wearing red print specialty shop beach pajamas with solid red trim. *Jackie Rovick Collection.*

OPPOSITE PAGE: Color Illustration 74. *Patsykins* with metal sleep eyes wearing her original dress and bonnet by Effanbee.

LEFT: Color Illustration 75. A later version of *Patsykins* with a larger eye cut and sleep eyes. She is wearing her all-original ensemble by Effanbee which has a natural waistline. *Nancy Carlson Collection. Photograph by David Carlson.*

ABOVE: Color Illustration 76. *Patsykins* with painted side-glancing eyes wearing her all-original party ensemble. *Judy Johnson Collection.*

BELOW: Color Illustration 77. *Patsyette* with painted side-glancing eyes wearing a specialty shop outfit labeled "Glad Togs." *Jackie Rovick Collection.*

RIGHT: Color Illustration 79. *Patsyette,* seen in *Color Illustrations 77* and *78,* in her undergarment. *Jackie Rovick Collection.*

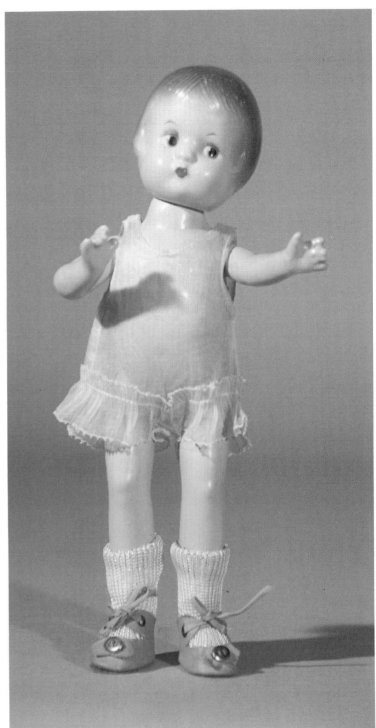

LEFT: Color Illustration 78. Back view of the *Patsyette,* seen in *Color Illustration 77,* showing the label on the back of the outfit. *Jackie Rovick Collection.*

RIGHT: Color Illustration 82. *Patsyette Twin Brother* wearing his original Effanbee suit with the gold paper heart-shaped tag on his wrist and standing with his original box.

BELOW: Color Illustration 81. Side view of *Patsyette*, seen in *Color Illustration 80*, showing the detail of the bonnet. *Billie Nelson Tyrrell Collection.*

RIGHT: Color Illustration 80. *Patsyette* with painted side-glancing eyes wearing her all-original party outfit by Effanbee. *Billie Nelson Tyrrell Collection.*

ABOVE: Color Illustration 84. Comparative view of an all-original *Patsyette* with painted eyes and hair and a *Patsyette* with painted side-glancing eyes and a mohair wig.

RIGHT: Color Illustration 83. *Patsyettes* with painted side-glancing eyes (one has them to the left and the other has them to the right). Both have bobbed mohair wigs and are wearing all-original Effanbee labeled costumes.

LEFT: Color Illustration 85. Bride and Groom *Patsyettes* in all-original Effanbee costumes. The pair came together in their own tan and brown box with the heart symbol. *Joyce Olsen Collection.*

RIGHT: Color Illustration 86. The tan and brown box with the heart symbol in which the Bride and Groom *Patsyettes*, seen in *Color Illustration 85*, came. *Joyce Olsen Collection.*

BELOW: Color Illustration 87. *Patsyette* with painted side-glancing eyes and a bobbed wig shown with her wardrobe trunk. *Karen Brownell Collection. Photograph by James Brownell.*

Color Illustration 88. *Patsyettes* as *Kit* and *Kat,* Dutch characters. Each came in a separate box. *Inge Simms Collection.*

ABOVE: Color Illustration 89. All-original black *Patsyettes* with painted side-glancing eyes and wearing party outfits. The doll on the left is dark brown and the one on the right is a light chocolate color.

RIGHT: Color Illustration 90. Rare version of *Patsyettes* as Hawaiian Royalty. The King displays his feather cloak while the Queen models her muumuu with its train. She is also wearing a coconut frond hat.

RIGHT: **Color Illustration 91.** Rare *Patsyette* portraying Hawaiian Royalty. She is shown wearing her muumuu with intertwined leis fastened to her head.

BELOW: **Color Illustration 92.** Side view of the rare *Patsyette* portraying Hawaiian Royalty, seen in *Color Illustration 91*, showing her train.

ABOVE: **Color Illustration 93.** Back view of the rare *Patsyette* portraying Hawaiian Royalty, seen in *Color Illustration 91* and *92*.

Color Illustration 94. *Patsyette* as a Hawaiian hula girl with intertwined leis fastened to her head and around her wrists and neck. The bandeau top part of her dress shows the Diamond Head print with the palm trees and she is wearing a natural grass skirt. *Lucia Kirsch Collection.*

PATSY WARDROBES FOR CHRISTMAS GIFTS

Illustration 213. These original advertisements from the 1932 *McCall Decorative Arts & Needlework* magazine show the patterns offered by the McCall Corporation, numbers 1918 and 1919 for *Patsy* in the 11½in (29cm), 14in (36cm), 16in (41cm), 19in (48cm) and 22in (56cm) sizes. These patterns are highly sought-after by collectors today. The patterns were said to fit *Blossom Peaches* as well, one of the competitive look-alikes.

1919

1918

No. 1919. A little flowered frock and an embroidered one with matching bonnet are only two out of six items in this charming outfit for Patsy doll. There is a flannel coat and hat to be worn over the flowered frock, then there is a stunning sailor suit with middy blouse and bloomers, and a gym suit, also a cunning set of underwear. These will fit a Blossom Peaches doll as well. Cutting pattern in sizes 11½, 14, 16, 19 and 22 inches, with full directions. 25 cents. Blue.

No. 1918. Patsy doll's mother adores the little gingham frock with the "good luck" elephant cross-stitched in front, it has a hat to match. And next, the little round yoked one of dotted swiss with embroidery. Other things in this chic outfit are a flannel coat and hat, a pajama ensemble and a set of underwear. Pattern in 5 sizes, 11½, 14, 16, 19 and 22 inches, 25 cents. Blue.

PATSY FAMILY IN THREE SIZES

PATSY FAMILY IN THREE SIZES

The famous Patsy family! With a pretty head of real human curly hair. How sweet she looks in her dainty silk dress and bewitching hair bow. She wears a little pantie combination and white socks and slippers. Strong composition body; movable arms, legs and head with sleeping eyes and lashes. Dress in Pink or Blue. **State color.** Sizes as follows:

No. 25/196—Patsy, 13"..............................$4.25
No. 25/197—Patsy Joan, 16"......................$5.00
No. 25/181—Patsy Ann, 19".......................$7.50

210

211

212

Illustration 210. 19in (48cm) *Patsy Ann*; all composition; human hair wig with bangs; wears her original pale blue organdy dress with a shirred lace-edged neckline, ribbon bows on the shoulders, French ribbon rosettes trim the ruffle edge on the front of the dress. Dolls with this style of hair were sold by F.A.O. Schwarz in 1935. *Inge Simms Collection.*

Illustration 211. 19in (48cm) *Patsy Ann*, seen in *Illustration 210*, in her original bloomer-shaped one-piece undergarment in pastel blue. A mended tear at the neck has been cleverly mended and disguised with cotton lace but it was originally plain. *Inge Simms Collection.*

Illustration 212. Original advertisement from the F.A.O. Schwarz 1935 Christmas catalog referring to the dolls as "The famous Patsy Family." Silk dresses for the 19in (48cm) *Patsy Ann* came in blue or pink and she had sleep eyes and real human curly hair with a different type of bow from the earlier bandeau.

SHIRLEY TEMPLE AND PATSY DRESSES

SHIRLEY TEMPLE CLOTHES

Ski Suit and Hat

Of soft suede-finish material, smart and toastywarm for little Shirley's outings into the snow. In Red, Green or Blue. **State color.**

No. D-973/1—For 13" Shirley.....$2.25
No. D-973/2—For 18" Shirley.....$3.00
No. D-973/3—For 22" Shirley.....$3.50

Raincoat Sets

Include coat, hat and umbrella of bright rubberized plaid. In Red or Green. **State color.**

No. D-311/1—For 13" Shirley.....$2.00
No. D-311/2—For 18" Shirley.....$2.25
No. D-311/3—For 22" Shirley.....$2.75

Serge Coat and Hat

For dressy wear. In Red or Blue.

No. D-986/1—For 13" Shirley.....$2.00
No. D-986/2—For 18" Shirley.....$2.75
No. D-986/3—For 22" Shirley.....$3.25

Plaid Dress with white top

No. D-154/1—For 13" Shirley.....$2.00
No. D-154/2—For 18" Shirley.....$2.75
No. D-154/3—For 22" Shirley.....$3.25

Party Dress. Pink or Blue

No. D-220/1—For 13" Shirley.....$1.75
No. D-220/2—For 18" Shirley.....$2.25
No. D-220/3—For 22" Shirley.....$3.00

Gingham Dress with Jacket. Pink or Blue

No. D-205/1—For 13" Shirley.....$1.50
No. D-205/2—For 18" Shirley.....$2.25
No. D-205/3—For 22" Shirley.....$2.75

NEW PATSY CLOTHES

Ski Suit and Hat

Designed just like Shirley's of the same soft suede finish fabric and comes in the same bright shades of Red, Green or Blue. **State color.**

No. D-973/4—For 13" Patsy......$2.50
No. D-973/5—For 16" Patsy Joan..$2.75
No. D-973/6—For 19" Patsy Ann...$3.00

Raincoat Sets

Also the same as Shirley's in vivid Red or Green plaids. Include coat, hat and umbrella. **State color.**

No. D-311/4—For 13" Patsy......$2.00
No. D-311/5—For 16" Patsy Joan..$2.25
No. D-311/6—For 19" Patsy Ann...$2.50

Serge Coat and Hat

In Red or Blue. **State color.**

No. D-986/4—For 13" Patsy......$2.25
No. D-986/5—For 16" Patsy Joan..$2.50
No. D-986/6—For 19" Patsy Ann...$3.00

Plaid Dress with white top

No. D-154/4—For 13" Patsy......$2.25
No. D-154/5—For 16" Patsy Joan..$2.50
No. D-154/6—For 19" Patsy Ann...$2.75

Party Dress. Pink or Blue

No. D-220/4—For 13" Patsy......$2.00
No. D-220/5—For 16" Patsy Joan..$2.25
No. D-220/6—For 19" Patsy Ann...$2.50

Gingham Dress with Jacket. Pink or Blue

No. D-205/4—For 13" Patsy......$1.75
No. D-205/5—For 16" Patsy Joan..$2.00
No. D-205/6—For 19" Patsy Ann...$2.25

214

Illustration 214. Original advertisement from the F.A.O. Schwarz 1935 Christmas catalog showing separate columns of similar clothing for the 13in (33cm), 18in (46cm) and 22in (56cm) *Shirley Temple* dolls and the 13in (33cm) *Patsy*, 16in (41cm) *Patsy Joan* and 19in (48cm) *Patsy Ann*. A ski suit and cap in suede cloth in red, green or blue was offered as well as raincoat sets. A serge coat, which appears to be a simplified version of one worn by Shirley Temple in *The Little Colonel* was also available as well as a gingham dress with a jacket, almost surely copies from one worn by Shirley in *Our Little Girl*. They were offered for the *Patsy* dolls as well.

TO PLEASE SMALL GIRLS AND BOYS

No. 243. These cunning clothes for a Patsy doll will please any little girl. The outfit includes an adorable smocked dress, a sweet dress with a frill edge, embroidered collar, a romper suit trimmed with cross-stitch, and a little raincoat and hat set. These clothes are just like those a little girl wears herself, even to the touches of dainty embroidery. For Patsy dolls 11½, 14, 16, 19 and 22 inches. Full directions. Yellow. Pattern, 25 cents.

215

Illustration 215. Original advertisement from *The New McCall Needlework Book* for 1935 shows pattern number 243 which was available for the 11in (28cm), 14in (36cm), 16in (41cm), 19in (48cm) and 22in (56cm) *Patsy* dolls with full directions. The clothes were said to be of the type a little girl wears herself, even to the touches of dainty embroidery. It included a smocked dress, a party dress, a romper suit and a raincoat and hat set. Most of the original Effanbee outfits were shorter than the outfits made from patterns.

Illustration 216. Original advertisement from *The New McCall Needlework Book* for Winter 1935 shows the smocked dress and the party dress which could be made from pattern number 243.

No. 243. This complete doll's wardrobe of four costumes, will delight the heart of any child. The party dress has an embroidered surplice collar, the play dress has matching panties. The two other costumes are a rainy-day outfit and a Russian smock. For Patsy dolls in sizes 11½, 14, 16, 19 or 22 inches. Yellow transfer. Pattern, 25 cents.

216

217

Illustration 217. The trade magazines
announced in February of 1935 that,
after many years on the ground floor at
Union Square, Fleischaker & Baum
had opened a showroom on the
ground floor in the Fifth Avenue
Building. Window displays were created for the buyers with valuable hints
for displays to be made by the dealer of
Effanbee dolls. A "moving picture" of
these displays was said to be available
and would illustrate the progress of
the American doll industry. It is not
known whether *Patsy Bright Eyes*, advertised as the newest member of the
Patsy family, was the first with the
glassene eyes or was a tie-in with the
Bright Eyes movie made in 1934 with
Shirley Temple. This advertisement is
from *Toys and Novelties* magazine for
March 1935.

Doll Clothing

Doll's Clothes for Shirley Temple and Patsy Ann	
Cloth Coat and Hat—Trimmed with fur, hat to match, BLUE or RED. State color.	
No. D-983/1—For 18 inch Shirley	$3.00
No. D-983/2—For 22 inch Shirley	3.75
No. D-983/3—For 19 inch Patsy Ann	3.50
Raincoat Sets—Include coat, hat and umbrella of bright rubberized plaid. In RED or GREEN. State color.	
No. D-311/1—For 18 inch Shirley	$2.25
No. D-311/2—For 22 inch Shirley	2.75
No. D-311/3—For 19 inch Patsy Ann	2.50
Ski Suit and Hat—Of soft suede-finish material, smart and toastywarm for little dolly's outing into the snow. In RED or BLUE. State color.	
No. D-973/1—For 18 inch Shirley	$3.00
No. D-973/2—For 22 inch Shirley	3.50
No. D-973/3—For 19 inch Patsy Ann	3.00
Pajamas—Checked Flannel one piece Pajama. In PINK or BLUE. State color.	
No. D-505/1—For 18 inch Shirley	$ .85
No. D-505/2—For 22 inch Shirley	1.00
No. D-505/3—For 19 inch Patsy Ann	.85
Wool Red Plaid Skirt with White Dotted Swiss Blouse.	
No. D-535/1—For 18 inch Shirley	$2.75
No. D-535/2—For 22 inch Shirley	3.25
No. D-535/3—For 19 inch Patsy Ann	2.75
Figured Print Jumper Dress, Colored Lawn Blouse, glass buttons. In Red or Blue. State color.	
No. D-0362/1—For 18 inch Shirley	$1.25
No. D-0362/2—For 22 inch Shirley	1.50
No. D-0362/3—For 19 inch Patsy Ann	1.50
White Dotted Swiss Dress, trimmed with PINK or BLUE. State Color.	
No. D-492/1—For 18 inch Shirley	$2.25
No. D-492/2—For 22 inch Shirley	2.75
No. D-492/3—For 19 inch Patsy Ann	2.25

218

Illustration 218. F.A.O. Schwarz designed and created exclusive outfits in
its own studios in addition to selling
Effanbee dolls in their original factory
outfits. After the debut of the *Shirley
Temple* doll, some outfits were also
made to fit the 18in (46cm) and 22in
(56cm) *Shirley Temple* dolls as well as
the 19in (48cm) *Patsy Ann*. This original advertisement is from the F.A.O.
Schwarz 1936 Christmas catalog.

Illustration 219. 19in (48cm) *Patsy
Ann* models a green plaid raincoat, cap
and umbrella which were all designed,
created and sold by F.A.O. Schwarz in
New York. White boots with slide fasteners were fairly new at this time.
The outfit was also available in red
plaid. *Martha Sweeney Collection.
Photograph by Martha Sweeney.*

219

Illustration 220. 19in (48cm) *Patsy Ann* dolls. *Patsy Ann* on the left models a specialty shop felt coat of lime green with darker green pink scallops, appliqued flowerets of pink, white, blue, red, lavender, yellow, tan and brown. *Patsy Ann* on the right also models a specialty shop tan felt coat with brown trim and flowerets of blue petals with pink centers sewn on with gold thread and green leaves.

Illustration 221. 19in (48cm) *Patsy Ann* models a teal blue felt coat with velvet trim and matching beret. *Janice Baughman Collection. Photograph by David Carlson.*

220

221

Illustration 223. Close-up of the 19in (48cm) *Patsy Ann*, seen in *Illustration 222*, showing the detail of the face. *Bothwell/Chapman Collection. Photograph by owner.*

222

223

Illustration 222. 19in (48cm) *Patsy Ann*; all composition; reddish-brown painted hair; blue tin sleep eyes, painted eyebrows, a closed mouth; wears a white dress with red polka dots with a solid red panel in front and on the skirt bottom, a white piqué collar trimmed in red with a matching piqué bonnet trimmed in red piping; dress is labeled on the back; gold paper heart-shaped tag on the wrist. This doll was advertised in 1936. *Bothwell/Chapman Collection. Photograph by owner.*

The Variants

In the 1930s and 1940s, the Effanbee Doll company had no perception whatsoever that they were creating future treasured heirlooms. The aim of the firm was to make high-grade toys for children to play with and to sell as many of them as possible.

The *Tousle Head* dolls were a series of various dolls in different sizes. They were not advertised as having individual names except for the general term "Tousle Head." Effanbee was so proud of the curly lamb skin wigs and emphasized the fact with the name *Tousle Head*. Had the manufacturers had any idea how much collectors would have liked to put a specific name on each doll, they would have gladly complied, at least in advertising, if not in the actual marking.

In *The Effanbee Patsy Family* (our self-published book, now out of print), we had presumed that "Little Sister" was the name given by Effanbee to the doll with the *Lovums* type head and the *Patsy Ann* torso. It appears this is merely a "catalog name" from the 1931 Sears, Roebuck and Co. to differentiate her from the "Tousle Head Baby" version. The doll was never intended to be an "open-mouthed *Patsy Ann*" — there is no such thing. We have since acquired advertising for the *Tousle Head* dolls in the F.A.O. Schwarz 1931 and 1935 Christmas catalogs. In the 1935 catalog, the name is spelled "*Tousel Head*."

In 1931, she was called a straight leg *Tousle Head* doll. The curly lamb skin wigs came in red, blonde or brown shades. Her silk dress was available in green, blue, red or pink. A rare 22in (56cm) size with a *Patsy Lou* torso was also available for $10.00.

At the same time, one could order a *Tousle Head* (*Lovums* type) baby doll with a red, brown or blonde tousle wig in the 22in (56cm) size for $10.00 or the 18in (46cm) size for $7.50.

The *Tousle Head* girl, using a *Patsy Ann* body, is one of the most realistic and radiant composition dolls ever created. Although she is very photogenic, one really needs to see the actual doll to realize her beauty.

Another *Patsy Ann* variant is the doll with the head marked "Mary Ann" but using the *Patsy Ann* body but she will be covered later as there are earlier *Mary Ann* versions as well with composition shoulder plates and cloth stuffed torsos.

New information has come to light in a 1932 Effanbee publication *My Doll's Magazine*. The *Tousle Head* dolls on *Patsy* torsos were named "The Bettys." She is not mentioned herein, but the *Tousle Head* variant in the *Patsy* chapter with the head mold of *Patsy Babykin* was evidently the smallest *Betty*. Mentioned in *My Doll's Magazine* are 16½in (42cm) *Betty Brite*, 19in (48cm) *Betty Bounce* with a *Patsy Ann* torso and 22½in (57cm) *Betty Bee* with a *Patsy Lou* torso. The real lamb skin wigs came in blonde, red or brunette hues. The clothing was mentioned as beautiful silk or dotted swiss frocks.

224

225

Illustration 224. 19in (48cm) *Tousle Head Betty Bounce* using the *Patsy* torso and the *Lovums* mold head; all composition; green glassene eyes, real hair upper eyelashes, painted upper and lower eyelashes, open mouth with upper and lower teeth; wears original yellow cotton dress with a pleated skirt which was possibly made by the F.A.O. Schwarz company in its studios.

Illustration 225. Back view of the 19in (48cm) *Tousle Head Betty Bounce*, seen in *Illustration 224*, showing the body construction and the *Patsy* torso.

Illustration 226. This original advertisement from the Baltimore edition of the 1931 Sears, Roebuck and Co. catalog differentiates between "Little Sister Tousle Head" and "Tousle Head Baby" with its own designation of names which were not those given by Effanbee. The catalog artist has probably sketched the dress even shorter than it actually was. "Little Tousle Head" is shown wearing a scarlet silk crepe dress with a matching combination suit undergarment. This is the only all-composition doll which came with a locket and a chain. All Effanbee dolls with lockets had cloth bodies with this one exception.

TOUSLE HEAD
TRADE MARK REG

I Sleep
I Talk
18 In.
Tall

How would you like a dolly whose hair you could comb and brush? That's what you can do with these two little Tousle Heads for their wigs are REAL lamb skin with the silky hair just as it grew. These wigs are washable and fast color.

$4.89 $6.98

EFFANBEE
"The Doll with the Golden Heart"

I Sleep
19 In.
Tall

All Composition

226

Tousle Head Baby
A chubby, lovable Baby with sleeping eyes and real lashes. Beautifully modeled composition head turns in any direction on a swivel neck. Famous "Tousle Head" lamb skin wig. Composition arms and dimpled legs jointed at shoulders and hips. Cuddly kapok stuffed body and cry voice. Pink and white broadcloth rompers; white socks and bootees. 18 in. tall. Effanbee locket.
48 C 2599—Postpaid....**$4.89**

Little Sister Tousle Head
Head, body and limbs of finest composition with swivel neck, the famous tousle hair, sleeping eyes, real lashes. Jointed at shoulders and hips, Little Sister can take a hundred delightful, childish poses . . . she stands alone. Frock and pantie combination of scarlet silk crepe. White socks, red slippers. Effanbee locket and chain. 19 inches tall.
48 C 2596—Postpaid.. **$6.98**

"TOUSEL-HEAD" DOLL
No. 25/157—This is "Tousel-Head", adorable as can be. So wide-awake, she keeps looking up at you out of her bright eyes but then she closes them when the Sandman calls her into the "land o' nod." She's a mass of curly locks—and the softest, silkiest you ever did see because the wig is finest curly lambskin, and what's more it's washable—little mothers can shampoo it. She's wearing panties, socks and slippers and her pretty dress can be ordered in Blue or Red check. State color. Doll, 19" tall................**$6.75**

228

Illustration 228. In 1935, F.A.O. Schwarz offered a 19in (48cm) *Tousle Head* doll for $6.75 in its Christmas catalog. Note that the original advertisement spelled the name "Tousel-Head." The doll's chin and arm have been outlined by an artist so they will "stand out" more in the catalog. Interestingly, the tousle wig was advertised as "...washable — little mothers can shampoo it." One shudders to think what would happen to the composition if a child attempted this.

134

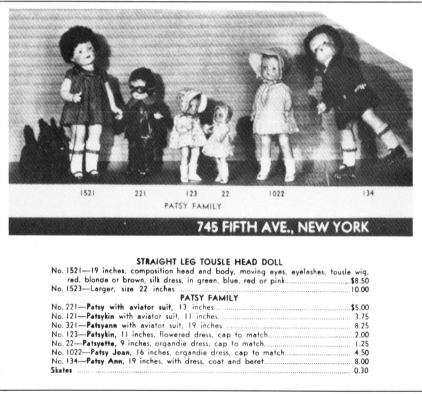

PATSY FAMILY

745 FIFTH AVE., NEW YORK

STRAIGHT LEG TOUSLE HEAD DOLL
No. 1521—19 inches, composition head and body, moving eyes, eyelashes, tousle wig, red, blonde or brown, silk dress, in green, blue, red or pink.............................$8.50
No. 1523—Larger, size 22 inches 10.00

PATSY FAMILY
No. 221—**Patsy** with aviator suit, 13 inches..$5.00
No. 121—**Patsykin** with aviator suit, 11 inches 3.75
No. 321—**Patsyann** with aviator suit, 19 inches 8.25
No. 123—**Patsykin**, 11 inches, flowered dress, cap to match.................................2.00
No. 22—**Patsyette**, 9 inches, organdie dress, cap to match..................................1.25
No. 1022—**Patsy Joan**, 16 inches, organdie dress, cap to match............................4.50
No. 134—**Patsy Ann**, 19 inches, with dress, coat and beret....................................8.00
Skates 0.30

227

Illustration 227. Original advertisement from the F.A.O. Schwarz 1932 Christmas catalog gives the name "Straight Leg Tousle Head Doll" to the *Patsy Ann* variant, shown on the left, which came with a red, blonde or brown tousle wig. This deluxe version in a silk dress of green, blue, red or pink cost $8.50. The 22in (56cm) version using the *Patsy Lou* body cost $10.00. The *Patsy* shown second from the left, number 221, is wearing an F.A.O. Schwarz version of an aviator suit, a rare item never seen. Amazingly, *Patsy Ann's* roller skate shoes cost $.30!

230

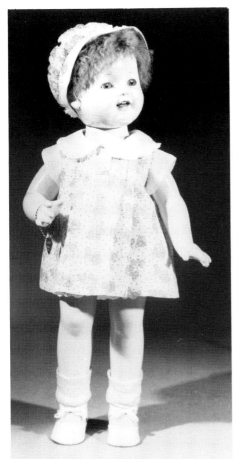

229

Illustration 229. 19in (48cm) *Tousle Head Betty Bounce* with lamb skin wig using the typical *Patsy Ann* body and the *Lovums* type head. She has green glassene eyes and the special mouth treatment with four upper and four lower teeth and a tongue which give her an older appearance. The dress she wears is blue and white corded dimity with a white woven crossbar dimity bonnet brim, collar and cuffs. She also wears replaced shoes and socks. *Judy Johnson Collection.*

Illustration 230. Close-up of the 19in (48cm) *Tousle Head Betty Bounce*, seen in *Illustration 229*, showing the detail of the face. Note the very "alive" expression of the doll. *Judy Johnson Collection.*

Illustration 231. 19in (48cm) *Tousle Head Betty Bounce* with the *Lovums* type head and the *Patsy Ann* marked body; rich brown tousle lamb skin wig with full original curl; sleep eyes, painted and real hair upper eyelashes, painted lower eyelashes, upper and lower teeth, molded tongue; wears original organdy dress with a white bound cotton collar, puff sleeves, deep hem. *Nancy Carlson Collection. Photograph by David Carlson.*

Illustration 232. Close-up of the 19in (48cm) *Tousle Head Betty Bounce*, seen in *Illustration 231*, showing the detail of the face. Note that the modeling under the eyes, cheeks and mouth give the doll a very realistic appearance. *Nancy Carlson Collection. Photograph by David Carlson.*

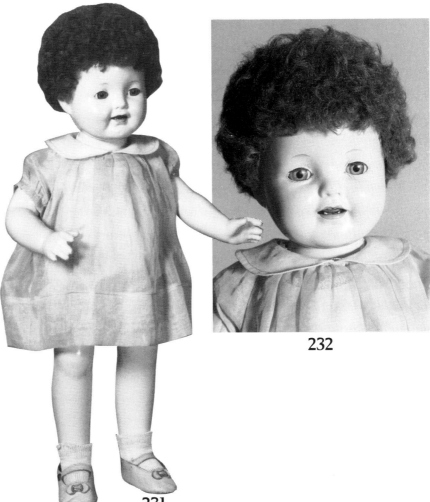

231

232

Chapter Six

Patsykins,

A Smaller Sister

It is a bit difficult for collectors to think of a doll which is clearly marked "Patsy Jr." as being actually named *Patsykins* (in other words "little *Patsy*"). Effanbee was very flexible and open to new ideas and decided "*Patsy Jr.*" sounded too boyish and even though molds had been made with that name, "*Patsy Jr.*" was officially dropped.

The earliest mention of *Patsykins* comes under a paragraph in *Toys and Novelties* magazine for February 1930 under the heading "Effanbee News:"

"The great success of Patsy and Patsy Ann has resulted in the introduction of a new number of this famous 'Irish' doll family — for Patsykins, a smaller sister, as it were, has made her appearance and bids fair to duplicate the popularity of her larger sisters. In Patsykins, Fleischaker and Baum present a little doll packed full of personality, offered in a wide variety of dainty dressings. She is only one of many newcomers promised by this house."

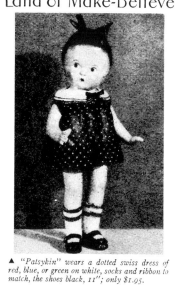

In the Children's Land of Make-Believe

▲ *"Patsykin" wears a dotted swiss dress of red, blue, or green on white, socks and ribbon to match, the shoes black, 11"; only $1.95.*

234

Illustration 233. In the April 1930 issue of *Toy World* magazine Fleischaker & Baum announced the debut of *Patsykins* (marked "Patsy Jr" on the torso). The doll is so new that she is not yet illustrated. *Patsy Ann*, with the gold paper heart-shaped tag on her wrist is shown, as is a prototype of *Lovums* with painted eyes and a metal heart-shaped necklace (which came on the mama dolls and some large babies).

Illustration 234. In the December 1930 issue of *Good Housekeeping* magazine, under the title "In the Children's Land of Make-Believe," *Patsykins* makes her debut, but her name is spelled "Patsykin" and she was marked "EFFANBEE//PATSY JR//DOLL" on the torso. She wears a simple little dress of dotted swiss which came in red, blue or green and her socks and hair ribbon match the dress. Her shoes are black. She was 11in (28cm) and sold for $1.95.

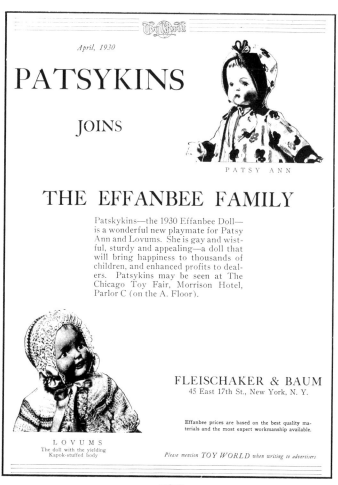

April, 1930

PATSYKINS

JOINS

PATSY ANN

THE EFFANBEE FAMILY

Patskykins—the 1930 Effanbee Doll—is a wonderful new playmate for Patsy Ann and Lovums. She is gay and wistful, sturdy and appealing—a doll that will bring happiness to thousands of children, and enhanced profits to dealers. Patskykins may be seen at The Chicago Toy Fair, Morrison Hotel, Parlor C (on the A. Floor).

LOVUMS
The doll with the yielding Kapok-stuffed body

FLEISCHAKER & BAUM
45 East 17th St., New York, N. Y.

Effanbee prices are based on the best quality materials and the most expert workmanship available.

Please mention TOY WORLD *when writing to advertisers*

233

235

236

Illustration 235. 11in (28cm) *Patsykins*; all composition; painted reddish-brown hair; painted side-glancing eyes; wears all original clothing. This is an early 1930s version with the gold paper heart-shaped tag hanging from the wrist. There were no gold metal heart-shaped bracelet tags until 1932. Her undergarment is a one-piece combination suit with lace at the legs. *Nancy Carlson Collection. Photograph by David Carlson.*

Illustration 236. Close-up of the gold paper heart-shaped tag for the 11in (28cm) *Patsykins*, seen in *Illustration 236*, which reads: "This is//PAT-SYKINS//TRADE MARK PAT. PEND.//The Lovable Imp//with tiltable head//and movable limb//AN//EFFanBEE//DURABLE//DOLL." *Nancy Carlson Collection. Photograph by David Carlson.*

Full-page advertisements in March, April and May of 1930 announced: "The Birth of a New Playmate for Lovums and Patsy Ann, Patsykins — the 1930 Effanbee Doll — is a wonderful new playmate for Patsy Ann and Lovums. She is gay and wistful, sturdy and appealing — a doll that will bring happiness to thousands of children, and enhanced profits to dealers." No actual photograph of the newly featured doll is shown on these pages but *Patsy Ann* and *Lovums* are illustrated. This was to pique the curiosity of the buyer to come to the showroom.

Good Housekeeping magazine offered *Patsykins* for Christmas 1930. She is shown in a dotted swiss dress of red, blue and green with a white collar, a ribbon bandeau to match, socks and black shoes. This 11in (28cm) doll was priced at $1.95, which was $1.00 less than the cost of a *Patsy*.

The Christmas catalog from F.A.O. Schwarz for 1932 included a suitcase with *Patsykins* for $8.95. The case was ribbed black patent leatherette and had a handle and lock. *Patsykins* was said to fit inside nicely and was wearing either a pink or blue Effanbee outfit. The trousseau was an exclusive with Schwarz and included a printed cotton play dress with bloomers, a dainty figured dimity dress with bloomers and a hat, a nightgown, a romper suit, blue and white figured beach pajamas with a sun hat to match, a smart red woolen coat with gray krimmer collar and a krimmertrimmed beret to match, all for $8.75.

Patsykins was described as an adorable 11in (28cm) doll of almost unbreakable composition with movable eyes, head and limbs. The first version had painted eyes.

Among the rarest to locate would be a *Patsykins* in an original Spanish, Uncle Sam or Dutch costume designed by the F.A.O. Schwarz firm. These came in individual boxes and cost $4.50, more than double the cost of the separate doll which was $2.00. Some of these possibly still exist but have not been recognized as being authentic.

At Christmas in 1933, Marshall Field & Co. offered an 11in (30cm) *Patsykins* and a 14in (36cm) trunk for $10.00. The wardrobe contained a school and party dress, a coat, a hat, crepe pajamas, a bathrobe, two handkerchiefs, shoes, socks, a washcloth, a towel and soap.

As late as December of 1938, *Good Housekeeping* magazine was offering a complete unsewn trousseau for *Patsykins* although the doll is not so named. This was probably done to make the trousseau seem suitable for other similar dolls as well. The actual doll does not seem to be offered.

Under the headline "MAKE CLOTHES FOR YOUR DOLLY — KNIT A BOLERO," from the December 1938 *Good Housekeeping* magazine, was the following story:

"Look at the lovely surprise we have for you! An adorable doll's trousseau to make, complete with undies, slip, nightie, bathrobe, play and party dresses, sunsuit and matching sunbonnet. Each little garment in the set comes in a separate transparent envelope, with necessary trimmings and illustrated instructions for making. The sections are cut, all ready to put together, and the most troublesome part of the sewing is finished. The designs and materials have been chosen for their adaptability to dolls' patterns and simple sewing, the trimmings specially made to sew on small curves easily. The sleeves are set in where necessary. All you have to do is turn the hem, sew up the seams, join the waist and skirt, put on the trimmings and fastenings, and — presto! — the garments are finished. Everything will fit to perfection, and you'll be surprised how quickly these things will grow in your hands. They are fun for you to make — or even for your small daughter, if she can sew a little. And how proud she will be of this beautiful trousseau for her favorite doll! The outfit is easily made by hand, but add a small sewing machine, and her happiness will be supreme. With

237

Illustration 237. A close-up of the marking on the back of a *Patsykins* doll: "EFFANBEE//PATSY JR// DOLL." The "Jr." was dropped as it was considered too boyish.

238

Illustration 238. A personalized gold metal heart-shaped bracelet tag which reads: "EFFANBEE//PATSY//KIN." The original gold paper heart-shaped tags read "Patsykins" with an "s" at the end, but this tag reads "PATSY// KIN" and the name is broken simply because there was not enough space to put it all on one line. Other dolls seem to have the bracelet tags which were not personalized, yet they appear to be original. There were no gold metal heart-shaped bracelet tags until 1932.

Illustration 239. 11in (28cm) *Pat-sykins*; all composition; brown painted hair; blue-gray metal sleep eyes, painted lower eyelashes, real hair upper eyelashes, a tiny rosebud mouth; wears original corded dimity dress with flower design, piqué bonnet brim and dress collar with touches of hand embroidery, lace on the bonnet, collar and sleeves, replaced shoes. *Louise Kopfer Collection.*

Christmas and its frenzy of preparations just ahead, what could be more opportune!

"Dolls and dolls' clothes are thrilling gifts for little girls, while bigger girls delight in making pretty clothes for their favorites. Busy mothers haven't time to spend on elaborate dolls clothes', and often they are not sufficiently skillful with needle to instruct a child in the fine art of needlework. Nor is sewing required in the curriculum of every school; yet it is essential that every girl, large or small, should know how to sew. Given this outfit all cut out and ready to sew, the child-mother, concerned for her doll-child's appearance with 'not a thing to wear for the holidays,' will set to work with enthusiasm. It will be fun for her to make miniature copies of her own pretty clothes.

"Won't you let us send you a trousseau for that doll you are planning to dress for your little girl, and another to slip into a well-equipped sewing basket for her little sister?"

This was probably the last promotion for extra wardrobes for the *Patsy* dolls. Among the many firms manufacturing clothes or other accessories for the *Patsy* family dolls in the early 1930s were M. L. Kahn in New York, Fred K. Braitling in Bridgeport, Connecticut, and Gladys G. Myers in Seattle, Washington. Gladys Myers' advertisement read: "*Glad Togs* for the Patsy Family, Latest Styles, Original, Fast Selling."

Illustration 240. Side view of the 11in (28cm) *Patsykins*, seen in *Illustration 240*, showing the detail of the bonnet. *Louise Kopfer Collection.*

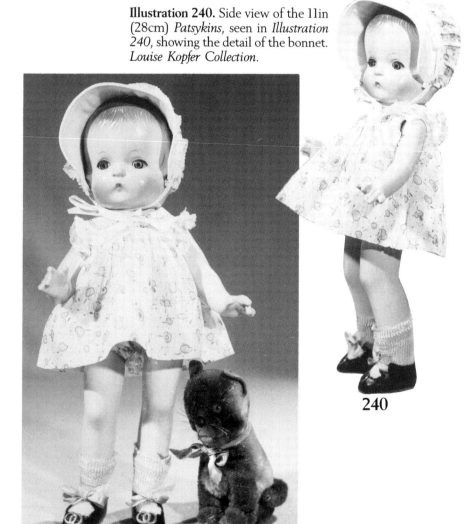

240

239

SUITCASE WITH
PATSYKIN

242

Illustration 242. Advertisement from the F.A.O. Schwarz 1932 Christmas catalog, under the title "DOLLS AND THEIR WARDROBES, All of Superior Quality," showing *Patsykins* (listed as "Patsykin") with a suitcase. The copy read as follows:

"No. A-181/11—Patsykin's very attractive suitcase that will carry the doll and her things. The case is ribbed black patent leatherette and has a handle and lock. Patsykin fits in nicely and wears a pretty blue or pink outfit when you first see her. Besides this, the suitcase holds a printed cotton play dress with bloomers, a dainty figured dimity dress and bloomers with hat, a nightgown, a romper suit, blue and white figured beach pajamas with a sun hat to match, a smart red woolen coat with gray krimmer collar and a krimmer trimmed beret to go with it. Patsykin is the adorable 11" doll of almost unbreakable composition with movable eyes, head and limbs. State color, pink or blue. Complete......$8.75."

Note the key for the case tied to the handle with a satin ribbon. The doll's bonnet brim is turned back to better reveal her petite face.

241

FANCY DRESS TROUSSEAUX

No. A-2/60/5

No. A-2/60/5—Here are three fancy dress costumes to set off the charms of the delightful 11½" **Patsykin** doll.

Dutch costume—Dress with plain blue top and kerchief—a peaked Dutch Bonnet, a pretty nosegay and wooden shoes.

Uncle Sam costume—Red and white striped trousers with star trimmed blue flare. Blouse is white with red, white and blue on tie, and vestee blue, with white stars. Striped cap.

Spanish costume—Yellow sateen sleeveless dress, blue sateen piped in yellow for the jacket, a chenille fringed, figured silk shawl with rose and a black sateen hat.
Three costumes, without dolls, in box.............................$4.50

Patsykin Doll, extra..$2.00

243

Illustration 241. 11in (28cm) *Patsykins*, with sleep eyes, in a blue trunk with a wardrobe. Some of the garments are made from the McCall patterns.

Illustration 243. Advertisement from the F.A.O. Schwarz 1932 Christmas catalog which showed three exclusive Schwarz costumes listed as "FANCY DRESS TROUSSEAUX." Note that the doll is called "Patsykin" rather than *Patsykins*.

244

Illustration 244. Original advertisement from Marshall Field & Co. for Christmas 1933 showing a *Patsykins* and her trunk. This appeared under the headline "Fashions Of The Hour, Santa Claus Suggests..." and shows a child wearing a broadcloth dress copied from one worn by Princess Elizabeth with a linen collar and cuffs and metal buttons.

The doll with the trunk was listed as number 4229. The trunk contained a school and party dress, a coat, a hat, crepe pajamas, a bathrobe, two handkerchiefs, shoes, socks, a washcloth, a towel and soap. The doll was 11in (28cm) in a 14in (36cm) trunk and the complete set cost $10.00.

Marshall Field & Co. of Chicago, Illinois, carried the finest toys and probably assembled this trunk set "in-house" as did F.A.O. Schwarz.

Illustration 245. 11in (28cm) all-original *Patsykins*; painted hair; gray-blue metal sleep eyes, painted lower eyelashes, real hair upper eyelashes, a rosebud mouth; wears a pink organdy lace-trimmed Effanbee outfit with a separate batiste slip and lace-trimmed combination suit; marked on torso: "EFFANBEE//PATSY JR//DOLL." Note her gold metal heart-shaped bracelet tag which reads: "EFFANBEE//DURABLE//DOLL." *Inge Simms Collection.*

245

Illustration 247. Comparative view of three versions of *Patsykins*. They are, left to right: a version with blue-gray metal sleep eyes and eyelashes, a version with a mohair wig and painted side-glancing to the right eyes and a version with painted hair and extra large painted side-glancing to the left eyes. All are marked on the torso: "EFFANBEE// PATSY JR//DOLL."

Illustration 248. 11in (28cm) *Patsykins*; painted hair with a wig added; wears an outfit of blue and white cotton piqué like material handmade from McCall's pattern number 1919. She is wearing replaced shoes.

247

246

Illustration 246. Side view of the 11in (38cm) all-original *Patsykins*, seen in *Illustration 245*, showing the detail of the rosette-trimmed bonnet and the gold metal heart-shaped bracelet tag which dates her from 1932 or later. *Inge Simms Collection.*

248

250

249

251

Illustration 249. 11in (28cm) black *Patsykins*; all composition painted dark brown; three black cotton thread pigtails fastened inside the head which has three holes drilled for them; painted side-glancing eyes appearing as hearts on their sides, a rosebud mouth; wears her original bloomer combination suit; marked on the torso: "EFFANBEE//PATSY JR//DOLL." A few black *Patsykins* were made without the pigtails. Both are rare and much sought-after. The black *Patsykins* has a baby sister, *Patsy Babykins*, and there is also a black *Grumpykins* with three pigtails. Since there appears to be no advertising whatsoever on these choice items, they may have been made up for "special order." Note the gold metal heart-shaped bracelet tag which dates the doll from 1932 or later. *Inge Simms Collection.*

Illustration 250. 11in (28cm) black *Patsykins*, seen in *Illustration 249*, shown wearing her original Effanbee garment of pink cotton with lace trim at the neck and sleeves. *Inge Simms Collection.*

Illustration 251. 11in (28cm) black *Patsykins* wearing her all-original red silk outfit with the Effanbee woven heart label, socks with red stripes and red shoes. *Linda Den Boer Collection.*

Illustration 252. 11in (28cm) rare black *Patsykins*; all composition painted dark brown; three black cotton thread pigtails fastened inside the head; painted side-glancing eyes appearing as hearts on their sides, a rosebud mouth; wears her original home-sewn cotton print dress with touches of embroidery, real leather slippers by the Fred K. Braitling Company; marked on the torso: "EFFANBEE//PATSY JR//DOLL." *Atha Kahler Collection.*

Illustration 253. Close-up of the 11in (28cm) rare black *Patsykins*, seen in *Illustration 252*, showing the detail of the eyes and the pigtails. *Atha Kahler Collection.*

254

Illustration 254. Advertisement from the June 1932 issue of *Toy World* magazine for "Glad Togs" for the *Patsy* family by Gladys G. Myers of Seattle, Washington.

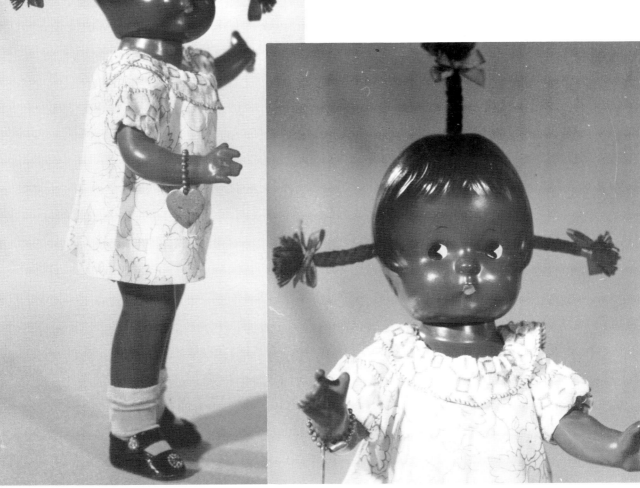

252

253

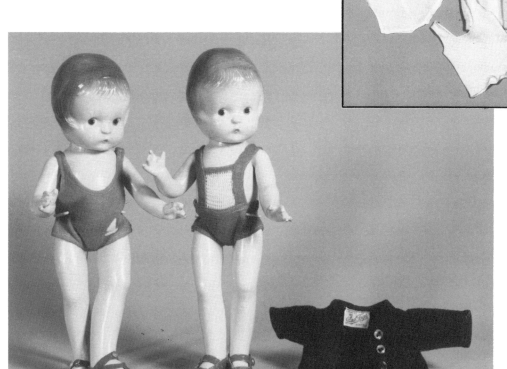

257

Illustration 257. Commercial undergarments and a pink and white bathrobe for the 11in (28cm) *Patsykins. Nancy Carlson Collection. Photograph by David Carlson.*

255

Illustration 255. Two 11in (28cm) *Patsykins* dolls wearing red wool bathing suits of wool jersey. The suit on the doll on the left has a sailboat on it and is labeled "CREATED//BY//Glad Togs//SEATTLE." The navy jersey sweater on the far right is also labeled "CREATED//BY//Glad Togs//SEAT-TLE." *Nancy Carlson Collection. Photograph by David Carlson.*

Illustration 256. Two 11in (28cm) *Patsykins* dolls. The one on the left is wearing an original Effanbee white cotton dress with blue polka dots, a caramel-colored silk-lined fur coat with silk covered buttons, a fur and velvet hat and caramel-colored leather shoes. The *Patsykins* on the right is wearing an original Effanbee white and red dotted swiss dress, a navy coat and beret labeled "CREATED//BY//Glad Togs//SEATTLE" and red leather shoes. This doll is wearing the gold paper heart-shaped tag. *Nancy Carlson Collection. Photograph by David Carlson.*

256

Illustration 258. Beach pajamas and a bathing suit for the 11in (28cm) *Patsykins*, both labeled "CREATED//BY//Glad Togs//SEATTLE." The sandals are original. The pajamas have large lavender, blue and salmon circles and are bound in green bias tape. *Nancy Carlson Collection. Photograph by David Carlson.*

Illustration 259. Outfits for the 11in (28cm) *Patsykins* dolls, left to right: a blue and white cotton checked print dress with white trim accents and button trim and a matching bonnet; a dress of pink and green designs on a white background and a white bonnet with matching trim and a pink and white dotted swiss party dress with lace trim and a matching bonnet. *Nancy Carlson Collection. Photograph by David Carlson.*

258

Illustration 260. The two 11in (28cm) *Patsykins* dolls, seen in *Illustrations 255* and *256*, standing with a full wardrobe of clothing. *Nancy Carlson Collection. Photograph by David Carlson.*

259

260

261

262

Illustration 262. Close-up of the back of the 11½in (29cm) all original *Patsykins*, seen in *Illustration 262*, showing the construction of the bonnet which buttons in the back and the marking on the back of the doll: "EFFANBEE//PATSY JR//DOLL." *Nancy Carlson Collection. Photograph by David Carlson.*

Illustration 261. 11½in (29cm) all original *Patsykins* with blue-gray glassene sleep eyes which are cut larger than the earlier tin eyes, giving the face a very wistful expression. She is wearing a dress with a full gathered skirt in a floral design which matches the material of the bonnet. The white crossbar dimity blouse was trimmed with dark ribbon in lace beading. *Nancy Carlson Collection. Photograph by David Carlson.*

Illustration 263. 11in (28cm) *Patsykins* shown in the December 1938 issue of *Good Housekeeping* magazine surrounded by her trousseau which could be purchased cut and partially sewn for convenience. Each garment came in a transparent envelope with trim. It is not known if any of these have survived.

Doll clothes cut and ready to put together—for you or a child to make

263

Chapter Seven

Patsyette,
A Still Smaller Sister

Illustration 264. Full-page advertisement from the February 1931 issue of *Playthings* magazine with the first mention of *Patsyette*, declaring her to be the newest in the Effanbee *Patsy* doll line.

Illustration 265. Introductory advertising for *Patsyette* from the May 1931 issue of *Playthings* magazine showing eight dolls in eight different versions of clothing including a Red Riding Hood costume and play and party fashions.

In January of 1931, the full-page Effanbee advertisement in *Playthings* magazine carried a message of appreciation to all the firm's friends and clientele and to all those who helped the firm's progress by their generous cooperation. Effanbee promised to continue to merit confidence by adhering strictly to past policy, "Quality Dolls at Popular Prices," and advised buyers to inspect its line in New York and look forward to seeing "The New Doll Hit of 1931." No name was given.

By February of 1931, another full-page advertisement showed a heart-shaped tag lettered: "EFFanBEE//DURABLE//DOLLS." Beneath that, the ad showed the message: "OUR HAPPY 'Patsy Families' are the High Spots in Doll News. Costumed in rare effects of color, texture and design, these dolls bespeak the latest styles in their Easter Finery. They truly excite an admiration that forecasts another tremendous demand for Patsy Ann, Patsy, Patsykins and Since trade preference commends our course 'Patsyette' Newest of the Patsy Line is but the natural outcome of foresight and advance planning. FLEISCHAKER & BAUM Creators of DOLLS THAT ARE DIFFERENT."

264

265

Patsyette now has been given a name. The four dolls were listed again in the headlines in March of 1931.

Toys and Novelties magazine for October 1931 ran a photograph of little Carol Bayard posing as a *Patsyette* doll in a parade in September in Ocean City, New Jersey. Her float had a raised platform for her to stand on with a rounded back marked "Patsyette." On the front and sides of the decorated float were many *Patsy* dolls wearing bathing costumes, the same as Carol. Her mother owned Carol's Kiddie Shop which probably sold *Patsy* dolls.

Playthings magazine carried a full-page illustrated advertisement for *Patsyette* and read: "PATSYETTE The Newest of the Patsy Family...." There were eight dolls illustrated. In the top row the dolls shown are one in a Red Riding Hood outfit, one in a sateen figured dress with a lace-edged collar and *Brother* and *Sister* twins in school outfits with matching berets. The second row shows dolls in two versions of party dresses (one with a plain yoke and lace at the neck and sleeves and another with a frilled or pleated collar), one in a checked percale school dress with a white collar and yet another in a party dress with a ruffle on the skirt bottom and a matching bonnet. The dolls without bonnets or berets wore ribbon bandeaus. At this time they wore light or dark slippers all fastened on the side.

In October 1931, *Toy World* magazine carried a full-page advertisement for "The Patsyette Twin Ensemble," said to be "The Newest Effanbee Sensation." What a delight for a child whose parents could afford it. The copy read:

"The Patsyette Twin Ensemble has already proved that depression does not exist when the goods are *right*.

"The Twin Ensemble consists of Brother and Sister Patsyette dolls and two complete changes of costume for each doll, packed in a flat carrying case with handle. Each change is a complete ensemble, including everything from hat to shoes. The case not only makes an exceptional display but is especially designed to make it easy for a child to carry. Nothing is lacking to make the Patsyette Twin Ensemble the most complete and satisfactory doll item ever offered to the trade — and advance sales have already proved

Illustration 266. The F.A.O. Schwarz 1931 Christmas catalog showed this rare oval-shaped box, 13in (33cm) by 6in (15cm), with a 9in (23cm) *Patsyette* dressed doll. Her wardrobe included two dresses with hats to match, beach pajamas, a coat and hat — all for $5.00. The doll came in an original Effanbee dress and the extra outfits were made in the Schwarz studio.

Illustration 267. 9in (23cm) *Patsyette* with extra large brown painted eyes, wearing a pink Effanbee dotted swiss outfit with a satin ruffle at the neck and satin ribbon trim at the skirt top. She is shown in her original box with four poses of the *Patsy* doll on the lid. The doll is wearing the gold metal heart-shaped bracelet tag which dates her from 1932 or later.

500 PATSYETTE TROUSSEAU

266

267

that it rings the bell with buyers, parents and children alike. Fleischaker & Baum, Creators of Dolls That Are Different."

By November of 1931, *Good Housekeeping* magazine offered to mail a 9½in (24cm) *Patsyette* in a pink or blue percale costume with a plain collar and a bow at the neck for $1.25. This smaller doll would be more affordable to many coping with the great financial Depression. Well in advance of Christmas, Frederick & Nelson department store in Seattle, Washington, ran a large advertisement in *Juvenile* magazine in August of 1931 declaring:

"All the Dollies Are Rejoicing! 'Patsyette' Has Come to Town.

"She's the tiniest, most lovable baby girl in the whole big Patsy-doll family — the dollies are having a party to welcome her. She can't decide whether to wear the red checked frock or the pink organdie. See all the other cunning clothes, made just for her! 'Patsyette' is only $1.25 in the Toy Shop, Fifth Floor."

F.A.O. Schwarz in New York appealed in general to an affluent clientele and for Christmas of 1932, offered three deluxe versions of *Patsyette* toys designed and made up in the firm's own studio.

Entitled "DRESSMAKERS," the catalog description for the first set reads: "A new idea! In a gaily colored box is a Patsyette doll 9" tall, surrounded by sufficient material to make a complete trousseau. This set includes figured and plain batistes, needles, thread, scissors, thimble, tape measure and all types of trimming, buttons, etc. Exclusive with F.A.O. Schwarz...$5.00." The outline of various paper patterns folded into the lid of the box cover can be seen.

Another deluxe set was offered by F.A.O. Schwarz for Christmas of 1932 entitled "NURSE OUTFIT." The catalog description reads: "Patsyette as a nurse, with a 5" enameled carriage and a cunning celluloid baby doll in long clothes. The nurse's uniform is of crisp blue and white with nurse's cap. There is a dainty sleeveless dress, a bonnet with ribbon, a figured dress with white collar, figured flannel pajamas and a soft pink jacket and beret. Outfit without doll...$4.95. Patsyette Doll, extra...$1.25."

Illustration 268. Advertising for *Patsyette* in the August 1931 issue of *Juvenile* Magazine for the Seattle, Washington, department store Frederick & Nelson. The sketches, which are accurate depictions of the Effanbee outfits for the doll, include a tailored coat and beret, a wool swimsuit, a robe and slippers, a party dress and bonnet and a play dress.

Illustration 269. The November 1931 issue of *Good Housekeeping* magazine advertised *Patsyette* as follows: "For the girl who loves a little doll, and is in pink or blue percale, full composition body, 9½", $1.25." The dresses ran longer in length than on the other dolls due to her smaller proportions.

All the Dollies Are Rejoicing! "Patsyette" Has Come to Town

She's the tiniest, most lovable baby girl in the whole big Patsy-doll family—the dollies are having a party to welcome her. She can't decide whether to wear the red checked frock or the pink organdie. See all the other cunning clothes, made just for her! "Patsyette" is only $1.25 in the Toy Shop, Fifth Floor.

Seattle, Washington   Frederick and Nelson

268

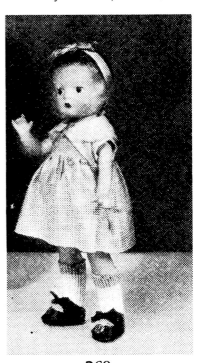

269

Illustration 270. 9in (23cm) *Patsyette* with olive brown side-glancing eyes, wearing an Effanbee pink organdy party dress and bonnet with ribbon rosette trim and lace trim at the neck and sleeves, a combination suit and slip of pink cotton and brown leather sandals by the Fred K. Braitling Company.

270

A third more elaborate item for the same year was listed as "WARDROBE TRUNK WITH NURSE DOLL." The catalog description reads: "How convenient to have a pretty Nurse doll, a jointed celluloid baby doll in long clothes and a cunning enameled carriage and all the nurse's things packed so nicely into a wardrobe trunk. The trunk, measuring 12½" high, 6¼" deep and 9" long when opened, is covered with brown imitation leather and has two real locks. Opens in front and top lifts up. Nurse doll, of almost unbreakable composition, with movable head and limbs, is dressed in a blue and white uniform with English style cap. The wardrobe contains a white flower printed dress and cap, a figured play dress, figured flannel pajamas, a flannel jacket and cap...$7.50."

Another rare item one might dream of finding intact was described in the catalog as "FANCY DRESS TROUSSEAUX." The catalog stated that *Patsyette* has had three lovely fancy dress costumes designed to fit her. The description reads:

"Shepherdess Dress — Flower figured pink and white dress with overskirt edged with pleated pink ruffles, over a plain pink front panel with black velvet bows. The pink bonnet has flowers under the brim and long brown curls attached. Black mask included.

"Hungarian Costume — A white cotton dress with rows of gold, blue and red ribbon around bottom. Sleeveless coat of light blue velveteen with white fur edge. Close fitting red cap. Long white silk stockings.

Illustration 272. 9½in (24cm) all-original *Patsyette Twin Brother*, wearing a red and white cotton play suit and a matching beret with a gold paper heart-shaped tag on his wrist. Effanbee did not bother to make separate tags for the *Brother* versions of the various *Patsy* dolls.

272

271

Illustration 271. Full-page advertisement from the October 1931 issue of *Toy World* magazine for "THE PATSYETTE TWIN ENSEMBLE." Note that the dolls have only the gold paper heart-shaped tags at this time. The company used the same *Patsyette* tag for both boys and girls.

Illustration 273. 9in (23cm) *Patsyette Twins* in original Effanbee blue and white matching cotton suits, blue shoes and socks with matching stripes. This outfit also came in red and white or green and white. *Judy Johnson Collection.*

Illustration 274. 9in (23cm) *Patsyette Twins* with brown painted side-glancing eyes looking towards each other. They are wearing specialty shop outfits. The dress is very cleverly made so it opens out completely when unbuttoned. No label remains on either outfit. *Linda Den Boer Collection.*

"Dutch Costume — Blue and white checked skirt with plain blue blouse. White kerchief and apron, white Dutch bonnet. Wooden shoes. The three costumes without dolls displayed in box...$3.50. Patsyette Doll, extra...$1.25."

One group of highly sought-after *Patsyettes* are the dark brown painted Hawaiians. There are several possibilities such as the king in his gold feather cloak, the lady in a muumuu and coconut frond hat or the version in the muumuu with a long train. Probably this model was intended to depict royalty.

The first legislature in Hawaii was opened by King Kamehameha III in 1845. His throne was covered with a feather war cloak and two large kahili (feather standards) towered over it. Young students at the Polynesian Center on Oahu explain to tourists that the King's hat represents the waning moon. The feathers for the King's cloak were plucked from a rare bird and often a King's cloak was not yet complete in his own lifetime.

There is no advertising by Effanbee on these dolls which were purchased "to special order" and dressed in Hawaii as souvenir dolls. One place where they are known to have been sold was the Liberty House which sold *Patsy* dolls and *Skippy* dolls as well.

273

274

Illustration 275. 9in (23cm) *Patsyette* dolls. The dolls on the left have brown painted side-glancing eyes to the left while the doll on the right has brown painted side-glancing eyes to the right. They are wearing, left to right, a hand-sewn dress, hand-sewn beach pajamas and an Effanbee gingham dress from 1931. *Rhoda Gage Collection.*

275

Illustration 276. 9in (23cm) *Patsyette* with brown painted side-glancing eyes, modeling a specialty shop garment of pink organdy with cotton Val lace at the neck, sleeves and on the full skirt. Underneath she wears a slip and combination of cotton batiste.

276

277

Illustration 277. 9in (23cm) *Patsyettes*. The one on the left is a rare doll with brown hair and two-toned blue eyes and is wearing a blue combination suit and her original blue shoes. She is missing her dress. The doll on the right has reddish brown hair and extra large brown eyes. She is wearing her red and white print dress with a white piqué collar with touches of embroidery and a scalloped ruffle on the collar.

Illustration 278. Back view of a 9in (23cm) *Patsyette* showing her yellow and red print dress with the label which has a gold heart with red lettering and which reads: "EFFanBEE// DURABLE//DOLLS [in the heart]" and underneath "MADE IN U.S.A." These labels do wash well and do not fade. They do ravel and can be backed by ribbon or pellon to preserve them. *Beth Bell Collection.*

Illustration 279. Back view of a 9in (23cm) *Patsyette* showing a simple cotton print blue and white dress with the printed satin label which has a gold heart with red lettering and which reads: "EFFanBEE//DURA-BLE//DOLLS [in the heart]." This type of label ravels very easily and should be removed before laundering, when necessary. The label can be backed with pellon for preservation. *Beth Bell Collection.*

278

279

281

Illustration 282. 9in (23cm) *Patsyette* with brown hair and extra large painted eyes. She is wearing a blue dotted dress which has a Molly-'es label and has her gold metal heart-shaped bracelet tag on her wrist.

280

Illustration 280. 9½in (24cm) *Patsyette*; reddish-brown painted hair; brown painted side-glancing eyes; wears a pink organdy dress with hemstitching trim on the skirt and bottom edge, matching pouf bonnet with hemstitching trim, separate pink cotton slip and combination undergarment, no labels. This is possibly a specialty shop creation. *Inge Simms Collection.*

Illustration 281. Side view of the 9½in (24cm) *Patsyette*, seen in *Illustration 280*, showing the detail of the pouf bonnet with the frill around the face. *Inge Simms Collection.*

Illustration 283. 9in (23cm) *Patsyette*; red-brown painted hair; olive brown painted side-glancing eyes; wears a pink organdy dress and bonnet with hemstitched ruffles, a one-piece slip and combination suit, dress (which is a specialty shop offering) is labeled: "Glad Togs, Seattle;" gold metal heart-shaped bracelet tag reads: "EFFanBEE//DURABLE//DOLLS." *Bothwell/Chapman Collection. Photograph by owner.*

282

283

153

284

285

Illustration 284. *Patsyettes* dressed as a wedding party. The Best Man on the left has light brown hair; the Groom has dark brown hair; the exquisite Bride has blonde hair and wears a white net veil and an embroidered organdy dress with a pannier hip effect and a picoted hem edge with ribbon flowerets at the waist; the Bridesmaid wears a peach brimmed hat with a flower, a glossy taffeta dress with panniers at the hip and an overskirt, a picoted hem edge and rosettes at the waist; the Minister has black hair and wears a surplice with a net tunic over his robes. It is unknown if these were dressed by Effanbee. *Ann Tuma Collection.*

Illustration 285. Back view of the *Patsyettes* in the wedding party, seen in *Illustration 284. Ann Tuma Collection.*

Illustration 286. 9½in (24cm) all-original *Patsyette Brother* as a Minister and part of a wedding group; black painted hair; brown painted eyes with black pupils; wears a full-length black robe, trousers, a white clerical collar, a lace and net cassock, *Patsyette* shoes and socks. *Chapman/Norwell Collection. Photograph by owner.*

286

154

Illustration 287. 9in (23cm) *Bridal Pair Patsyettes* which came in a divided Effanbee box. Both have brown painted side-glancing eyes. The Bride has light brown painted hair and wears a satin gown finished in hemstitching at the bottom, a net veil with a long train and ribbon trimmings at the sides of her face, carries her original bouquet of flowers with ribbon streamers and has her original pearls around her neck. The groom has black painted hair and wears a shirt, tie, vest, dark formal jacket and striped trousers. *Loraine Burdick Collection.*

Illustration 288. 9in (23cm) *Patsyette Bride,* seen in *Illustration 287. Loraine Burdick Collection.*

Illustration 289. Side view of the 9in (23cm) *Patsyette Bride,* seen in *Illustrations 287* and *288,* showing the detail of the cap and veil fastened under the chin with elastic. *Loraine Burdick Collection.*

288

289

291

Illustration 290. Volume 1, Number 3 of *The Patsytown News* from 1934 showed these *Dutch Twins*, special versions of *Patsyette*. The boy's cotton cap and shirt were red and the trousers were black. Red, white and blue were usually the colors used for clothing on the Dutch *Patsyettes*. These two dolls have blonde mohair wigs over molded hair. The *Patsy Tinyette Dutch Twins* are easier to locate than this set.

THE PATSYETTE TWINS

Just look at Miss Patsyette and her brother all dressed up in their Dutch Costumes ready for a Patsy Masquerade Party. Why don't you dress your Dollies up in fancy costumes and have a Patsy Masquerade for them? It's a lot of fun.

PATSYETTE TWINS

290

Illustration 291. 9in (23cm) all-original black *Patsyette* in a lovely milk chocolate color. She wears her all-original pink organdy Effanbee outfit with lace at the neck and sleeves, hem-stitched ruffle on the skirt bottom and a pink cotton combination suit and slip. *Judy Johnson Collection.*

Illustration 292. Comparative view of two 9in (23cm) black *Patsyettes* in two different styles of pink party dresses by Effanbee. The doll on the left is of a dark chocolate color while the doll on the right is a light milk chocolate color. Both have dark brown side-glancing eyes with black pupils. These are highly sought-after examples. Doll on the right, *Judy Johnson Collection.*

292

Illustration 293. 9in (23cm) dark brown *Patsyettes* portraying Hawaiian Royalty. Both dolls have black painted hair and brown painted side-glancing eyes. The doll on the left is wearing a muumuu and coconut frond hat. The doll on the right, intended to portray the King, has a cloak of feathers but is missing his hat.

Illustration 294. Back view of the 9in (23cm) dark brown *Patsyettes*, seen in *Illustration 293*, showing the feathered cloak on the doll on the left and the detail of the muumuu and hat on the doll on the right.

293

294

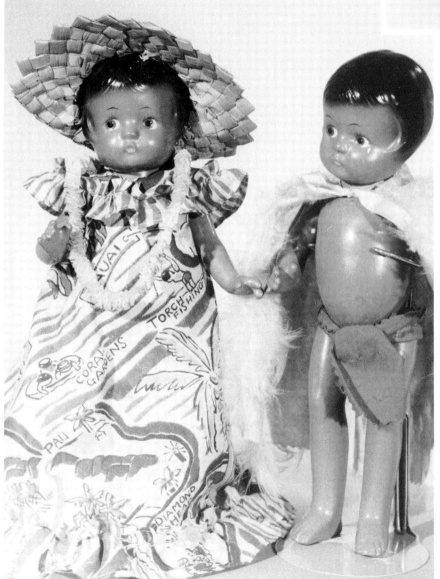

297

Illustration 295. 9in (23cm) black *Patsyette Brother* portraying a Hawaiian King. He has black painted hair and brown painted side-glancing eyes with black pupils. His yellow cotton moon-shaped hat was glued right on his head and is nearly always missing on this size and on the *Suzette Brother* version. He is also wearing a yellow feathered cloak and a brown figured cotton loincloth. *Beth Bell Collection.*

Illustration 296. Back view of the 9in (23cm) black *Patsyette Brother*, seen in *Illustration 295*, showing his "royal" cloak of yellow colored feathers. The shape of the hat symbolizes the waning moon. *Beth Bell Collection.*

Illustration 297. 9in (23cm) black *Patsyette* as a Hawaiian hula girl. She is painted a dark chocolate color. Intertwined leis are fastened to her head, which is painted black, and usually are missing. She has brown and black painted side-glancing eyes. The bandeau top part of her dress shows the Diamond Head print with the palm trees. She is wearing a natural grass skirt. These dolls were ordered undressed from Effanbee and were costumed in the Hawaiian Islands. They came with no known tags or labels. *Lucia Kirsch Collection.*

298

Illustration 298. Side view of the 9in (23cm) black *Patsyette*, seen in *Illustration 298*, showing the detail of the costume. *Lucia Kirsch Collection.*

295

296

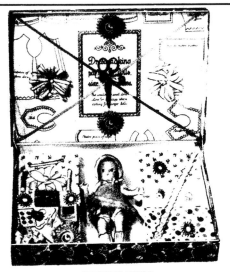

DRESSMAKERS

DRESSMAKERS

No. E-1026—A new idea! In a gaily colored box is a **Patsyette** doll, 9" tall, surrounded by sufficient materials to **make** a complete trousseau. This set includes figured and plain batistes, needles, thread, scissors, thimble, tape measure, and all types of trimming, buttons, etc. **Exclusive with F. A. O. SCHWARZ** $5.00

299

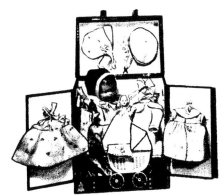

Wardrobe Trunk with Nurse Doll

WARDROBE TRUNK WITH NURSE DOLL

No. A-2/25/3—How convenient to have a pretty Nurse doll, a jointed celluloid baby doll in long clothes and a cunning enameled carriage and all the nurse's things packed so nicely into a wardrobe trunk. The trunk, measuring 12½" high, 6¼" deep and 9" long when opened, is covered with brown imitation leather and has two real locks. Opens in front and top lifts up. Nurse doll, of almost unbreakable composition, with movable head and limbs, is dressed in a blue and white uniform with English style cap. The wardrobe contains a white flower printed dress and cap, a figured play dress, figured flannel pajamas, a flannel jacket and cap .. **$7.50**

301

NURSE OUTFIT

NURSE OUTFIT

No. A-2/60/7—Patsyette as a nurse, with a 5" enameled carriage and a cunning celluloid baby doll in long clothes. The nurse's uniform is of crisp blue and white with nurse's cap. There is a dainty sleeveless dress, a bonnet with ribbon, a figured dress with white collar, figured flannel pajamas and a soft pink jacket and beret. Outfit **without** doll..$4.25
Patsyette Doll, extra...$1.25

300

Illustration 299. Original advertisement from the F.A.O. Schwarz 1932 Christmas catalog for a version of *Patseyette* called "DRESSMAKERS" which featured a 9in (23cm) *Patsyette* "surrounded by sufficient materials to make a complete trousseau." Patterns can be seen folded in the box lid. An original set has not yet been located.

Illustration 300. Original advertisement from the F.A.O. Schwarz 1932 Christmas catalog featuring a "NURSE OUTFIT" set which included a 9in (23cm) *Patsyette*, a 5in (13cm) enameled carriage and a celluloid baby doll.

Illustration 301. Original advertisement from the F.A.O. Schwarz 1932 Christmas catalog featuring an exceedingly rare "WARDROBE TRUNK WITH NURSE DOLL" set which included the 9in (23cm) *Patsyette* as a nurse with an enameled carriage and a celluloid baby doll packed in a wardrobe trunk with accessories.

Illustration 302. Original advertisement from the F.A.O. Schwarz 1932 Christmas catalog featuring "FANCY DRESS TROUSSEAUX" consisting of three different costumes available for the 9in (23cm) *Patsyette* doll. The costumes were for a Shepherdess Dress, an Hungarian Costume and a Dutch Costume. Schwarz also sold fancy dress costumes for children in this catalog. Effanbee also made the dolls in Dutch costumes.

302

EXQUISITE DOLLS,
MANY EXCLUSIVE WITH SCHWARZ,

No. A-2/60/4

FANCY DRESS TROUSSEAUX

No. A-2/60/4—Patsyette has had three lovely fancy dress costumes designed to fit her 9½" height.

Shepherdess Dress—Flower figured pink and white dress with overskirt edged with pleated pink ruffles, over a plain pink front panel with black velvet bows. The pink bonnet has flowers under the brim and long brown curls attached. Black mask included.

Hungarian Costume—A white cotton dress with rows of gold, blue and red ribbon around bottom. Sleeveless coat of light blue velveteen with white fur edge. Close fitting red cap. Long white silk stockings.

Dutch Costume—Blue and white checked skirt with plain blue blouse. White kerchief and apron, white Dutch bonnet. Wooden shoes. The three costumes **without** dolls displayed in box...$3.50
Patsyette Doll, extra...$1.25

Illustration 303. Advertisement for *Patsyette* at holiday time in a typical Effanbee party outfit, from an unknown newspaper dating from 1931.

Illustration 304. Advertisement from an unknown newspaper for a *Patsyette* in a party dress which originally sold for $1.25, now reduced to $.89. The paper mentions the dolls are nationally advertised and of the famous *Patsy* family. At this time, dolls did not come in sealed plastic packages as they do today and they would sometimes be shopworn, hence the bargain price.

SUMMER 1932

THE DOLL FASHION PARADE FEATURES SMART MINIATURE WARDROBES

10   10   10   10   10

10   10   10   10

No. 10. Dainty frilled frocks, bewitching bonnets, trig coat and hat, and even a flippant little sun suit and cuddly sleepers—what little girl wouldn't adore such a wardrobe for her Patsyette doll? These delightful little garments are designed to fit Patsyette, a doll only 9½ inches high, but they are actual little garments made just as a little girl's own clothes are—and they even have delicate touches of hand embroidery to give them a final chic finish. The dress at left is of yellow handkerchief linen with perky matching bonnet, trimmed in white organdy and hand embroidered. The "party" frock is of ecru lace over pink silk "undies". The peach pique sun suit is embroidered with fish and bubbles. The pink flanelette sleepers have a gay bird motif. The coat and beret outfit is of green flannel cunningly stitched, while the blue dotted swiss and organdy dress with its matching bonnet is embroidered in tiny sprays. Most little girls are delighted to learn to sew when they are making clothes for their Patsy dolls. Pattern for entire outfit, in one size only, 25 cents. (30 cents in Canada). Blue transfer.

305

Illustration 305. The *McCall Decorative Arts & Needlework* magazine for Summer of 1932 offered pattern number 10 for *Patsyette* exclusively, in one size only. The description reads as follows:

"No. 10. Dainty frilled frocks, bewitching bonnets, trig coat and hat, and even a flippant little sun suit [sic] and cuddly sleepers — what little girl wouldn't adore such a wardrobe for her Patsyette doll? These delightful little garments are designed to fit Patsyette, a doll only 9½ inches high, but they are actual little garments made just as a little girl's own clothes are — and they even have delicate touches of hand embroidery to give them a final chic finish. The dress at left is of yellow handkerchief linen with perky matching bonnet, trimmed in white organdy and hand embroidered. The 'party' frock is of ecru lace over pink silk 'undies'. The peach pique sun suit [sic] is embroidered with fish and bubbles. The pink flanelette [sic] sleepers have a gay bird motif. The coat and beret outfit is of green flannel cunningly stitched, while the blue dotted swiss and organdy dress with its matching bonnet is embroidered in tiny sprays. Most little girls are delighted to learn to sew when they are making clothes for their Patsy dolls. Pattern for entire outfit, in one size only, 25 cents. (30 cents in Canada). Blue transfer."

These outfits are exquisite and less seldom seen than other McCall designs.

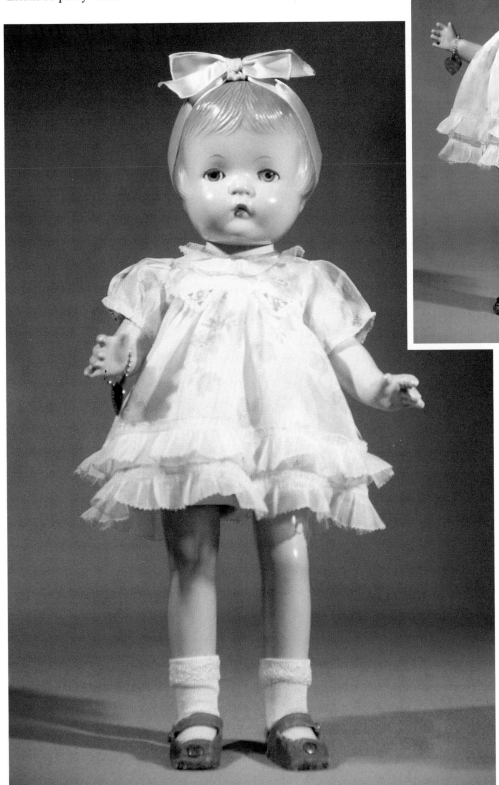

BELOW: Color Illustration 95. *Patsy Joan* with sleep eyes in her all-original Effanbee party frock.

ABOVE: Color Illustration 96. Side view of the *Patsy Joan*, seen in *Color Illustration 95*.

RIGHT: Color Illustration 100. *Patsy Joan* wearing a tailored checked cotton party dress with a piqué collar trimmed in organdy ruffles and a white piqué hat. *Jackie Rovick Collection.*

BELOW: Color Illustration 101. Side view of the *Patsy Joan*, seen in *Color Illustration 100. Jackie Rovick Collection.*

ABOVE: Color Illustration 102. *Patsy Joan* in an organdy party outfit by Effanbee. *Billie Nelson Tyrrell Collection.*

LEFT: Color Illustration 103. Side view of the *Patsy Joan,* seen in *Color Illustration 102,* showing the detail of the bonnet. *Billie Nelson Tyrrell Collection.*

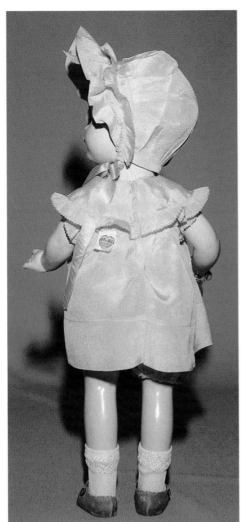

ABOVE: Color Illustration 104. Back view of a *Patsy Joan* wearing a labeled silk party outfit.

Color Illustration 105. A *Patsy Joan* from a trunk set models an Effanbee party dress while surrounded by the specialty shop wardrobe. *Hank Silvey Collection.*

LEFT: Color Illustration 106. Black *Patsy Joan* with black painted hair and brown sleep eyes. Her skin tone is a light chocolate color. *Joyce Olsen Collection.*

BELOW: Color Illustration 107. Close-up of the black *Patsy Joan*, seen in *Color Illustration 106. Joyce Olsen Collection.*

BELOW: Color Illustration 108. All-original *Patricia* with a wig models a tailored Effanbee print dress with a nautical touch on the collar. *Sherryl Shirran Collection.*

RIGHT: Color Illustration 109. Side view of the all-original *Patricia*, seen in *Color Illustration 108. Sherryl Shirran Collection.*

BELOW: Color Illustration 110. *Patsy Joan* in an all-original dress and bonnet by Effanbee. *Nancy Carlson Collection. Photograph by David Carlson.*

LEFT: Color Illustration 111. *Patsy Joan,* seen in *Color Illustration 110,* with her bonnet off. *Nancy Carlson Collection. Photograph by David Carlson.*

LEFT: Color Illustration 112. All-original *Patsy Joan* with a wig wearing a deluxe party ensemble. *Nancy Carlson Collection. Photograph by David Carlson.*

BELOW: Color Illustration 113. Back view of the all-original *Patsy Joan*, seen in *Color Illustration 112*, showing the detail of the bonnet and the NRA label on the Effanbee dress. *Nancy Carlson Collection. Photograph by David Carlson.*

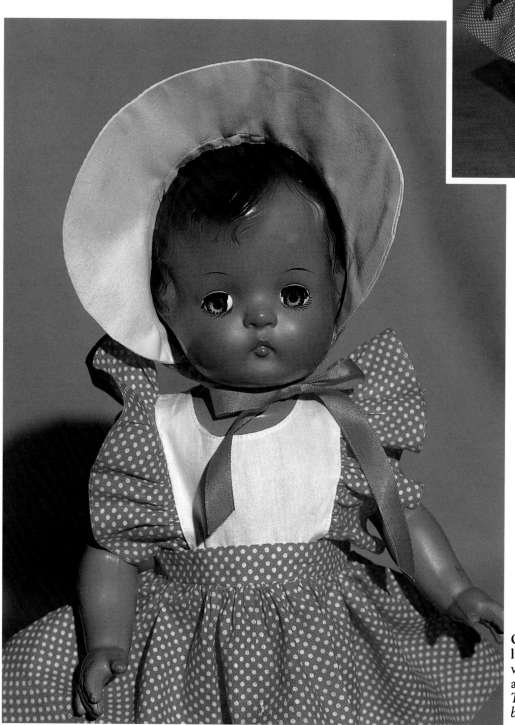

RIGHT: Color Illustration 114. All-original black *Patsy Joan* from the 1940s.

BELOW: Color Illustration 115. Close-up of the all-original black *Patsy Joan*, seen in *Color Illustration 114*, with her bonnet.

OPPOSITE PAGE: Color Illustration 116. *Patsy Lou* wearing her original sweater and pleated skirt. *Dorothy Tonkin Collection. Photograph by John Axe.*

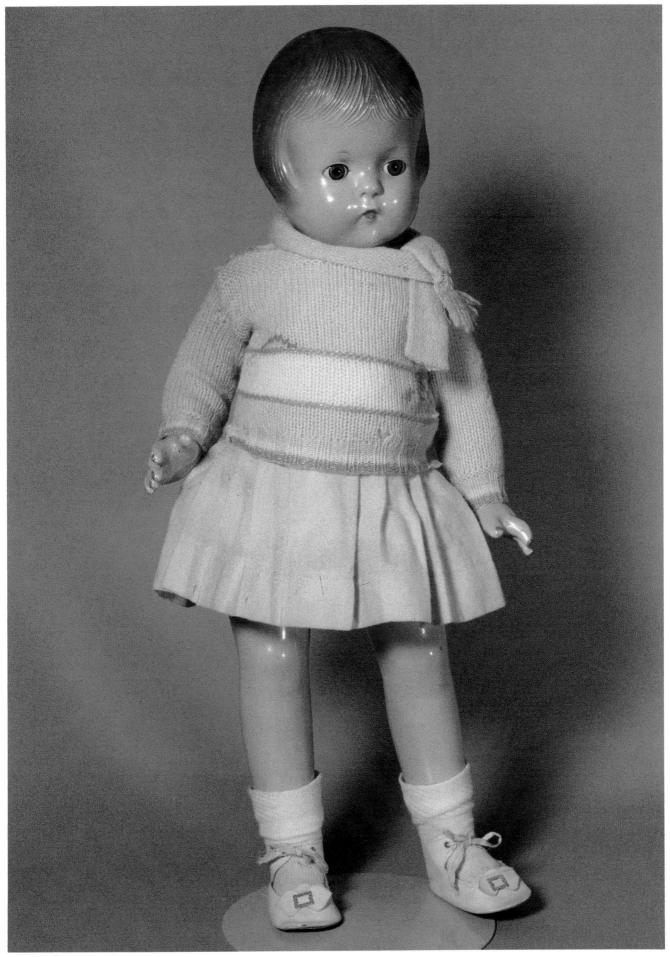

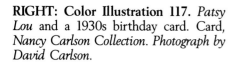

RIGHT: Color Illustration 117. *Patsy Lou* and a 1930s birthday card. Card, *Nancy Carlson Collection. Photograph by David Carlson.*

ABOVE: Color Illustration 118. Close-up of the 1930s birthday card, seen in *Color Illustration 117. Barbara Crescenze Collection. Photograph by John Axe.*

ABOVE RIGHT: Color Illustration 119. The inside of the 1930s birthday card, seen in *Color Illustrations 117* and *118. Barbara Crescenze Collection. Photograph by John Axe.*

LEFT: Color Illustration 120. *Patsy Lou* wearing her original flowered batiste dress with an organdy collar and a matching bonnet with a piqué brim.

BELOW: Color Illustration 121. Side view of the *Patsy Lou,* seen in *Color Illustration 120.*

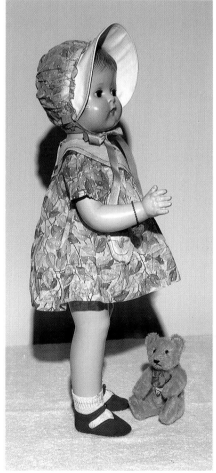

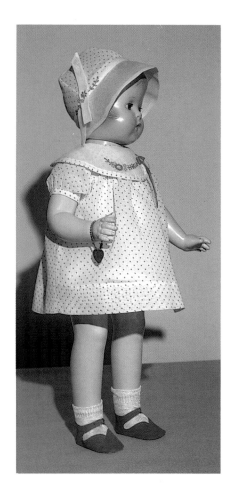

RIGHT: Color Illustration 122. *Patsy Lou* in an outfit sewn from a McCall pattern by the author's mother.

ABOVE: Color Illustration 123. Side view of the *Patsy Lou,* seen in *Color Illustration 122.*

ABOVE: Color Illustration 124. *Patsy Lou* wearing her all-original labeled Effanbee outfit. *Patsy Moyer Collection. Photograph by Patsy Moyer.*

LEFT: Color Illustration 125. Close-up of the *Patsy Lou,* seen in *Color Illustration 124,* showing the detail of her hat and her gold metal heart-shaped bracelet tag. *Patsy Moyer Collection. Photograph by Patsy Moyer.*

ABOVE LEFT: Color Illustration 126. Close-up of the gold metal heart-shaped bracelet tag on the *Patsy Lou,* seen in *Color Illustrations 124* and *125. Patsy Moyer Collection. Photograph by Patsy Moyer.*

306

309

307

308

Illustration 306. The *McCall Decorative Arts & Needlework* magazine for Winter of 1932 advertised pattern number 19 for *Patsyette Brother* with a headline "Patsy Wardrobes for Christmas Gifts." The description reads as follows:

"No. 19. Another enticing 'boy doll's' outfit is for a Patsyette doll, 9 inches high, and contains the little mannish suit and coat, the striped bathrobe and pajamas here shown, and a sun and sailor suit, also underwear. They are trimmed with tiny animals in simple outline, and the pattern is for one size only. Price, 25 cents. Blue. (30 cents in Canada.)"

Illustration 307. Comparative view of three 9in (23cm) *Patsyettes* with a blue trunk. They are all wearing beach pajamas and date from the 1930s. The doll on the left is wearing white cotton beach pajamas with a print collar. The center doll is wearing a one-piece silk garment with blue bands at the leg bottoms. The doll on the right is wearing multi-colored cotton print beach pajamas with red the dominant color, trimmed in red bias tape.

Illustration 308. 9in (23cm) *Patsyette*; red mohair wig; brown side-glancing eyes; wears a dress and bonnet of soft green batiste with a white collar trimmed in lace, matching undies; personalized gold metal heart-shaped bracelet tag reads: "EFFanBEE//PATSY//ETTE," dress label is sewn in front and has the gold heart with the red lettering which reads: "EFFanBEE//DURABLE//DOLLS [inside the gold heart]" and underneath "MADE IN U.S.A."

Illustration 309. Back view of 9in (23cm) *Patsyettes* showing the backs of their bonnets. The doll on the left is shown in *Illustration 308*, and has the label for the dress sewn on the front. The doll on the right is wearing a blue and white polka dotted batiste outfit with a white cotton collar with a scalloped edge and the dress label is sewn at the waist in back.

310

311

Illustration 310. 9in (23cm) *Patsyette* with a bobbed wig, wearing a felt coat and cloche hat with flower and leaf trim. She is also wearing a personalized gold metal heart-shaped bracelet tag. *Hank Levin Collection.*

Illustration 311. 9in (23cm) *Patsyette* with a bobbed wig, wearing a patterned print dress. She has painted side-glancing eyes and wears the gold metal heart-shaped bracelet tag which reads: "EFFanBEE//DURABLE// DOLLS." *Nancy Carlson Collection. Photograph by David Carlson.*

Illustration 312. 9in (23cm) *Patsyette* with a blonde mohair wig and painted side-glancing eyes. She is shown with a trunk and wardrobe. This doll has a hole in the top of the head for a wig knot, which was done in an earlier period on some dolls. *Photograph by James Brownell.*

312

313

Illustration 313. An entire family of *Patsyettes*, including boy and girl twins and girl twins. *John Axe Collection.*

Chapter Eight

Patsy Joan,
Beautiful Child

Illustration 314. The gold paper heart-shaped tag which came on *Patsy Joan's* wrist in 1931. It reads: "This is// PATSY JOAN//TRADE MARK PAT.PEND//The Lovable Imp//with tiltable head//and movable limb// AN//EFFanBEE//DURABLE// DOLL."

Illustration 315. Personalized gold metal heart-shaped bracelet tag for *Patsy Joan* which reads: "EFFanBEE// PATSY//JOAN." In 1932, these were used as well as the gold paper heart-shaped tags.

Patsyette, with her smaller size and consequently less expensive price, seems to have gotten the bulk of the attention in the trade magazines in the 1931 Depression days with full-page advertisements in May of 1931.

No special articles or photographs have been located in the trade magazines for *Patsy Joan* who was next in creation in the *Patsy* family. Fortunately, we also had our old catalog collection to share. *Patsy Joan* could be ordered from the 1931 F.A.O. Schwarz catalog as she came from Effanbee in an organdy dress with a cap to match, for $4.50. Although no colors are mentioned, the November 1931 *Good Housekeeping* magazine featured the same doll and mentions a choice of pink, blue, maize or green outfits.

F.A.O. Schwarz also offered its own 20in (51cm) high wardrobe with a 16in (41cm) *Patsy Joan* and two dresses, a coat and hat, a bathrobe, silk pajamas, a sweater and hat, beach pajamas, slippers, socks and roller skates, all for $20. For $5.00 less, the trunk, wardrobe and a 13in (33cm) *Patsy* were available.

The first version of *Patsy Joan* in a party dress was seen in the November 1931 issue of *Good Housekeeping* magazine under the heading "Santa Claus Land for Girls." She was shown with other Effanbee dolls. In the same issue was a page showing "Brother and Sister Dolls And Clothes You Can Make" featuring twin dolls in matching red and white cotton play outfits with matching berets.

The magazines offered pattern N-25 for a complete girl's trousseau for $.35 and pattern N-26 for a boy's wardrobe. We do not know if collectors have located these patterns as they were not distributed in as great a number as the more familiar McCall patterns.

Patsy Joan made her debut to the trade in the August 1932 issue of *Playthings* magazine with a full-page dramatic headline "HAVE YOU SEEN The NEW PATSY JOAN — THE FEATURE DOLL OF 1932."

A page from a notebook is sketched as though it was pinned to the magazine page with supposed comments from buyers who have seen this remarkable new Effanbee doll. Some of the comments are "Smart," "Lovable," "A Selling sensation" and "Just wait 'til the girls see her."

Regrettably (for the researcher), Effanbee begins the first of many advertisements with no photographs illustrating the doll in question. It appears the idea was to pique curiosity and get the buyers into the showrooms to actually see and, hopefully, order the dolls available.

Fortunately, a few photographs of the early versions of the doll have been preserved through advertisements in ladies' magazines which sold dolls or doll patterns by mail at this time.

The *Good Housekeeping* magazine for November 1932 featured *Patsy Joan* plus a pattern for her wardrobe under the heading "Dolls To Buy, and Clothes to Make." *Patsy Babykin* with a composition head and rubber body was also featured. The copy read: "Every little girl expects a doll Christmas morning, and here is Patsy Joan, a general favorite, with a tiltable head, movable limbs, and eyes that open and close. Her dress and teddy [combination suit] are made of green print, and her hat of green felt, white silk socks and kid slippers; 16 inches, dressed $3.95." *Patsy Joan* was $1.00 less expensive than the 19in (48cm) *Patsy Ann*.

In commenting on the pattern for *Patsy Joan, Good Housekeeping* magazine declared: "How mothers love to make dolls' clothes for their daughters as a surprise on Christmas morning! Above are trousseau patterns that fit Patsy Joan. Original in design, they include a coat and hat, ski costume, bathrobe, bathing suit, party dress and underclothes; pattern N-29 39 cents." None of these patterns have surfaced to date.

The *Patsy* dolls were often depicted as skiing, horseback riding, taking a trip on an ocean liner and so on — far beyond what the average little girl would be doing in this time period. This very well could have added to their panache and desirability.

Since it is never shown elsewhere, the riding habit illustrated in the F.A.O. Schwarz 1932 Christmas catalog for *Patsy Joan* is surely the firm's own design. (*Patsy* and *Patsy Ann* had similar outfits.) The copy read: "A smart riding habit that Patsy Joan, of the Patsy family, wears to perfection. She has thick-lashed, beautiful eyes which open and close delightfully. Her habit is red or tan and tailored of fine flannel with full breeches and a coat with wide lapels. A white shirt, soft riding habit and laced red leatherette puttees complete the ensemble, $6.50." The special outfit increased her basic $3.95 price more than half again.

Even more exciting in the same year was *Patsy Joan* in a silk dress — an Effanbee original. Then there were the original designs by F.A.O. Schwarz consisting of a caracul-trimmed coat and hat, a dress with a pleated skirt, a white fur coat and hat, a bathrobe, beach pajamas, a sweater and cap, extra shoes and roller skates, all for $20. Remember that the most inexpensive small composition doll sold for about $.25 at this time, so this was more expensive than we today would realize.

In December 1936, *Good Housekeeping* magazine offered a 16in (41cm) *Patsy Joan* for sale. She had "real hair, real eyelashes and really painted nails — the newest note" on these dolls. Her costume was red or blue plaid with a deep round organdy collar. Her hair was topped with a large plaid bow quite different from the original ribbon bandeau and her hair was said to come in either blonde or golden brown. The basic price increased to $4.95.

The *Patsy* dolls were very popular all through the 1930s, but eventually other personality dolls came on the scene. In 1946, *Patsy* and *Patsy Joan* were reissued and were still being sold in 1949.

Patsy Joan was 17in (43cm) tall and marked "Effandbee [with the 'd' added]" on the torso only, the only *Patsy* doll to be so marked. Her companion, a 1946 *Patsy*, was not marked at all. The arms of both dolls were slightly curved and the legs were well shaped.

There were white dolls with blue eyes and black dolls with brown eyes (which were described as "colored Patsy Joan" dolls) in the 1949 Effanbee catalog. Some models even had curled mohair wigs.

In the Sears, Roebuck and Co. 1950 Christmas catalog, *Patsy Joan* is listed as "Outdoor girl" and she is dressed to frolic in the sun in a cotton playsuit of assorted styles. This version was, no doubt, one of the very last of the composition dolls by Effanbee.

Illustration 316. Marking on the back of *Patsy Joan* which reads: "EFFanBEE//'PATSY-JOAN'." For unknown reasons, the marking on this doll is somewhat indistinct as compared to other dolls in the series.

316

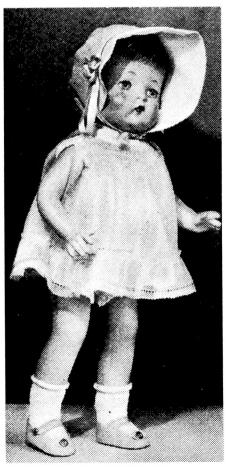

Illustration 317. This photograph of a 16in (41cm) *Patsy Joan* appeared under the heading "Santa Claus Land For Girls" in the November 1931 issue of *Good Housekeeping* magazine. She was described as wearing an organdy dress which was hemstitched and picoted with a frill and came with slippers, socks, lace-trimmed bloomers and a hat to match her frock. Her blue sleep eyes had real eyelashes. She could be ordered wearing a pink, blue, maize or green dress for only $3.95.

317

181

318

319

Illustration 318. This red-haired green-eyed *Patsy Joan* models a yellow organdy party dress with a matching bonnet. Her dress has pink shirring at the neck and pink hemstitching at the top of the yoke ruffle with similar trim in the body of the ruffle. The bonnet is trimmed with pink silk ribbon with a bow cluster at the side of the head. She wears matching cotton undergarments, silk socks with yellow stripes and her original shoes. This *Patsy Joan* dates from 1931. *Nancy Carlson Collection. Photograph by David Carlson.*

Illustration 319. For some unknown reason, Effanbee did not include special advertising for *Patsy Joan* in *Playthings* magazine in 1931. It may have been due to the great popularity of *Patsy Ann* and the company's desire to keep this going. Fortunately, *Good Housekeeping* magazine was selling the newer *Patsy Joan* by mail for Christmas in the November 1931 issue as shown here. Measurements in advertising often differed. The twins in this advertisement were listed as 16¾in (43cm) tall. The Effanbee costumes were red and white cotton with matching berets and the dolls were available for $3.95 each.

Illustration 320. The November 1931 issue of *Good Housekeeping* magazine which featured *Patsy Joan* and *Patsy Joan Twin Brother*, seen in *Illustration 319*, also featured two patterns — N-25 for a complete girl's trousseau including a coat, beret, bathrobe, beach pajamas, sleeping pajamas, a party dress and a teddy and N-26 for a boy's wardrobe including two suits (one for everyday and one for best), a gym suit, a bathing suit and sleeping pajamas. These patterns were available for $.35 each. At this time *Good Housekeeping* magazine conducted a shopping service and a pattern service.

320

321

323

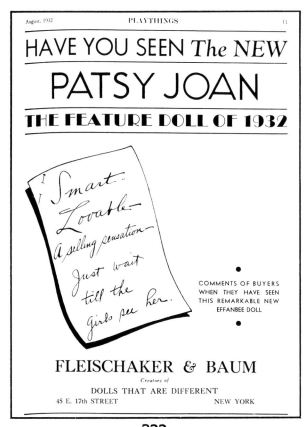

322

Illustration 321. 16in (41cm) *Patsy Joan Twin Brother* and *Patsy Joan* in green and white cotton outfits and matching green shoes. The boy's outfit has a silver buckle on his belt. These outfits also came in red and blue versions. The dolls have painted hair and green eyes and date from 1931. *Nancy Carlson Collection. Photograph by David Carlson.*

Illustration 322. Full-page advertisement appearing in the August 1932 issue of *Playthings* magazine for *Patsy Joan*. This demonstrates the Effanbee company's tendency to omit photographs of a new doll to entice the buyer into coming to view the product.

Illustration 323. The November 1932 issue of *Good Housekeeping* magazine did show a photograph of *Patsy Joan* who now comes with a gold metal heart-shaped bracelet tag, which can be seen on the doll, as well as a gold paper heart-shaped tag which is not shown. She is wearing a green print dress and teddy, a hat of green felt with a felt flower and leaf and rich satin ribbons to tie, as well as silk socks and slippers. She was available for $3.95. The trousseau pattern, N-29, included a coat and hat, a skiing costume, a bathrobe, a bathing suit, a party dress and dainty undergarments. It sold for $.35.

183

Illustration 324. 16in (41cm) *Patsy Joan;* reddish-brown painted hair; green eyes; wearing a green and white cotton print dress with a white piqué collar and cuffs and touches of hand embroidery on the collar. This is the same dress that is shown in the advertising photograph seen in *Illustration 323. Judy Johnson Collection.*

Illustration 325. In 1932, the F.A.O. Schwarz Christmas catalog offered *Patsy, Patsy Joan* and *Patsy Ann* in deluxe trunk sets. As shown here, *Patsy Joan* came in a 20in (51cm) trunk with trousseau and sold for $20 while *Patsy* came in a 16in (41cm) trunk with trousseau and sold for $15.

325

No. A-77—Trunk 20" with the 16" **Patsy Joan** Doll, including two dresses, coat and hat, bathrobe, silk pajamas, sweater and hat, beach pajamas, slippers, socks and roller skates........**$20.00**

No. A-76—Trunk 16" with 13" **Patsy Doll**, including two dresses, coat and hat, sweater and hat, beach pajamas, silk pajamas, bathrobe, slippers, socks and roller skates. All specially trimmed in our studio **$15.00**

CLOTHES FOR THE PATSY FAMILY

324

326

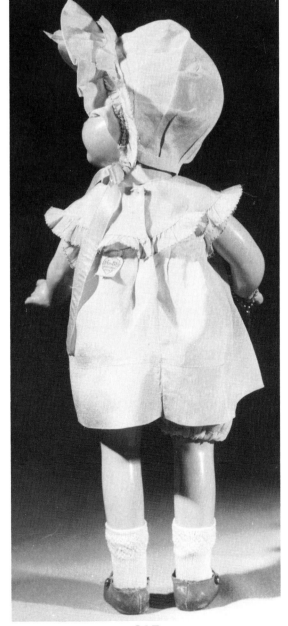

327

Illustration 326. 16in (41cm) all-original *Patsy Joan*; red painted hair; green eyes; wears a pale green silk party outfit with hand embroidery motifs on the deep ruffles collar and shirt, double flounce with hemstitching and gathers on the bonnet.

Illustration 327. Back view of the 16in (41cm) all-original *Patsy Joan*, seen in *Illustration 326*, showing the back of the dress and the detail of the bonnet. Note the woven label with the gold heart and the red lettering which reads: "EFFanBEE//DURABLE// DOLLS [within the heart]."

328

Illustration 328. An example of Effanbee's advertising from the May 1933 issue of *Playthings* magazine teasing the buyers into coming to see the "New and Novel Wonderland Costumes" but furnishing no photograph of the doll.

Illustration 329. 16in (41cm) *Patsy Joan* in the "Wonderland Costume" advertised in the May 1933 issue of *Playthings* magazine. She is wearing a yellow cotton flowered print dress with navy soutache braid on the skirt and a white cotton apron with ruffles over the shoulder. *Inge Simms Collection.*

329

331

330

332

Illustration 330. 16in (41cm) *Patsy Joan*, seen in *Illustration 329*, shown with a much earlier version of the "Wonderland Costume" on the cover of the book. *Inge Simms Collection.*

Illustration 331. Back view of the 16in (41cm) *Patsy Joan*, seen in *Illustrations 329* and *330*, showing the detail of the pinafore ruffles and the woven Effanbee label with the gold heart and the red lettering, sewn into the waist of the dress, which reads: "EFFanBEE//DURABLE//DOLLS [within the heart]" and underneath "MADE IN U.S.A." *Inge Simms Collection.*

Illustration 332. 16in (41cm) *Patsy Joan* seen in *Illustrations 329, 330* and *331*, wearing the correct combination undergarment for the 1933 "Wonderland Costume." *Inge Simms Collection.*

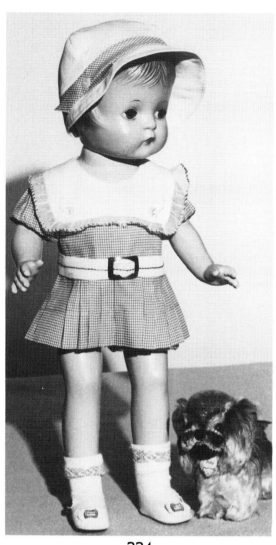

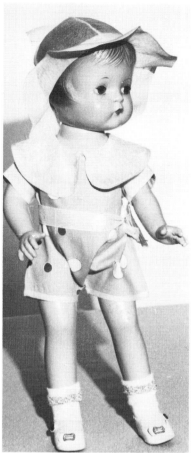

Illustration 335. All-original *Patsy Joan*, seen in *Illustrations 333* and *334*, wearing her organdy print playsuit and bonnet. *Hank Silvey Collection.*

334

Illustration 334. All-original *Patsy Joan*, seen in *Illustration 333*, wearing her Effanbee bloomer dress with a square yoke, button trim and embroidery on the ruffled collar. Note the detail of the hat trimmed with a bias cut checked band matching the dress. *Hank Silvey Collection.*

Illustration 333. An all-original *Patsy Joan* out of her trunk but surrounded by its contents. She is wearing her Effanbee bloomer dress and hat. The specialty shop creations include a dainty dotted swiss dress and bonnet with bloomers and an embroidered yoke, an organdy print playsuit and bonnet, a striped dress with a smocked collar, a panty and half-slip combination and a sheer batiste dress with a figured collar and bonnet. *Hank Silvey Collection.*

333

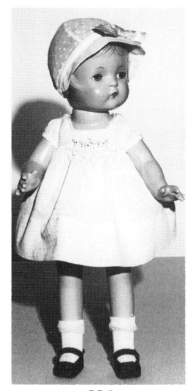

336

338

337

Illustration 336. All-original *Patsy Joan*, seen in *Illustrations 333, 334* and *335*, wearing her woven dotted swiss dress with blossoms and stems embroidered on the high yoke which also has several rows of smocking. *Hank Silvey Collection.*

Illustration 337. All-original *Patsy Joan*, seen in *Illustrations 333, 334, 335* and *336*, wearing her sheer batiste party dress with a figured collar and matching bonnet. *Hank Silvey Collection.*

Illustration 338. 16in (41cm) black *Patsy Joan*; painted light milk chocolate brown composition body; painted black hair; brown glassene eyes, dark painted eyebrows; wears a yellow crossbar dimity dress. *Joyce Olsen Collection.*

Illustration 340. 16in (41cm) *Patsy Joan*; reddish-brown painted hair; green glassene eyes, real hair upper eyelashes; wears an Effanbee pink flowered organdy dress with a double row of hemstitching ruffles at the bottom, a pink bonnet and socks with pink stripes. *Bothwell/Chapman Collection. Photograph by owner.*

Illustration 341. Close-up of the 16in (41cm) *Patsy Joan*, seen in *Illustration 340*, showing the detail of her hair, eyes and face. *Bothwell/Chapman Collection. Photograph by owner.*

342

Illustration 339. 16in (41cm) *Patsy Joan Brother* in an Effanbee multi-colored print top trimmed in tan felt with matching trousers. *Patsy Brother* had a similar outfit.

Illustration 342. 16in (41cm) *Patsy Joan* wearing a blue cotton dress with a white collar trimmed in blue braid with a red bow at the neck. This costume came with a felt hat similar to the one worn by the movie *Anne Shirley* doll. *Martha Sweeney Collection. Photograph by Martha Sweeney.*

339

340

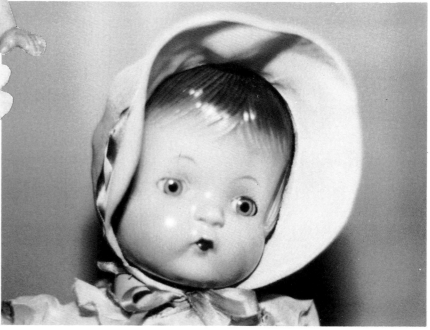

341

344

Illustration 344. The December 1936 issue of *Good Housekeeping* magazine showed this 16in (41cm) *Patsy Joan* with a side part with a large hair bow in her hair. She was available in a red or blue plaid dress with a deep organdy collar.

Illustration 345. All-original *Patsy Joan* wearing a print checked blue and white bloomer dress with a white piqué collar trimmed with pearl buttons in an embroidered design. The white belt has a silver colored buckle. The costume had a matching bonnet. *Nancy Carlson Collection. Photograph by David Carlson.*

159 160

160. Real hair, real eyelashes, and really painted nails—the newest note in a Patsy Joan doll dressed in red or blue plaid with hair bow to match; with blonde or golden brown hair; 16"; $4.95

Illustration 343. The F.A.O. Schwarz 1932 Christmas catalog advertised this riding habit for *Patsy Joan*. This exclusive outfit was made for *Patsy* and *Patsy Ann* as well in red or tan with leatherette puttees.

343

PATSY JOAN IN RIDING HABIT

PATSY JOAN IN RIDING HABIT

No. A-934/4—A smart riding habit that **Patsy Joan**, of the Patsy family, wears to perfection. She stands 16" tall of almost unbreakable composition, with jointed head, arms and legs. She has thick-lashed, beautiful eyes which open and close delightfully. Her habit is red or tan and tailored of fine flannel with full breeches and a coat with wide lapels. A white shirt, soft riding habit and laced red leatherette puttees complete the ensemble **$6.50**

No. A-934/3—Patsy, 13", dressed as above.. **5.00**

No. A-934/5—Patsy Ann, 19", dressed as above. **$7.50**

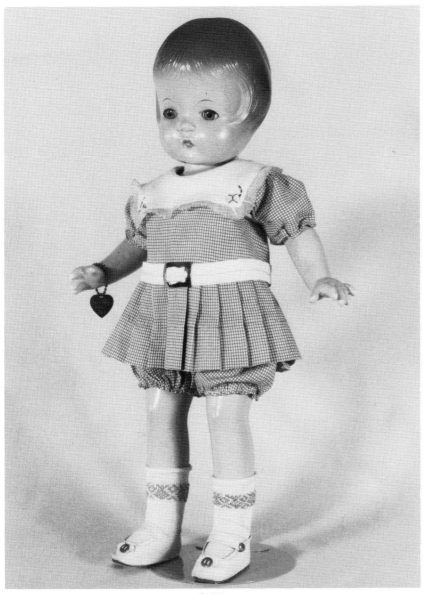

345

Illustration 346. Under the heading "Party Wardrobes For Christmas Gifts," the winter 1932 issue of *McCall Decorative Arts & Needlework* magazine showed *Patsy Joan* modeling "brother" styles of a woolly aviator suit and a short knit suit in pattern number 45, available for $.25. The same style was available for *Patsyette, Patsy, Patsy Ann* and *Patsy Lou.*

45   45

45. A wooly aviator suit and an abbreviated knit suit make valuable additions to every Patsy doll's wardrobe.

No. 45. (Left.) Not to have an up-to-date knitted suit or one of those snug aviator suits for Patsy doll is inexcusable these days. They are all the style, as you know, and the knitted one is so easy to knit from the careful directions and to fit by the pattern guide given. Adorable colors such as flesh, blue or pale green with white for the edges are very fetching. The other suit with 5-inch slide fasteners up the leggings is as cunning as can be in eiderdown. Two suits, sizes 11½, 14, 16, 19, 22 inches, with complete directions. Price is 25 cents. (30 cents in Canada.)

346

Illustration 348. 17½in (45cm) musical *Patsy Joan* variant; separate composition shoulder plate, cloth torso, composition arms and legs; brown painted hair; brown glassene eyes with eyelashes; wears her original blue and white lawn cotton dress with red piping on the collar and front yoke panel with three red covered buttons, white waffle pique brimmed bonnet edged in blue and white striped bias material to match the dress. *Nancy Carlson Collection. Photograph by David Carlson.*

Illustration 349. Back view of the 17½ in (45cm) musical *Patsy Joan* variant, seen in *Illustration 348.* Note the separate shoulder plate. The type of arms and legs which were ordinarily used in an all-composition elastic-strung doll have been adapted to fit the cloth torso. This enabled a music box to be inserted into the torso. *Nancy Carlson Collection. Photograph by David Carlson.*

(C)   **WIND ME UP and I'll play you a tune**

She stands by herself, 17½ in. high, and plays you a tune with her concealed 18-note Swiss music box! She is a beautiful new character doll, like a charming American girl; fully jointed arms and legs. She wears a cute frock over lovely underwear; white socks and slippers; adorable bonnet with silk ribbon bow tie. Around her wrist is a golden finished heart-shaped locket. When you put her to bed, she closes her eyes with their real lashes and goes to sleep. When you want her to entertain you, just wind her up and she'll play you a merry tune!

N26455   PRICE..............$8.40

347

Illustration 347. Original advertisement from the 1940 John Plain catalog for a musical *Patsy Joan,* although she was not advertised under her name. This doll is considered a rare version or a variant as it used the *Patsy Joan* head.

348

349

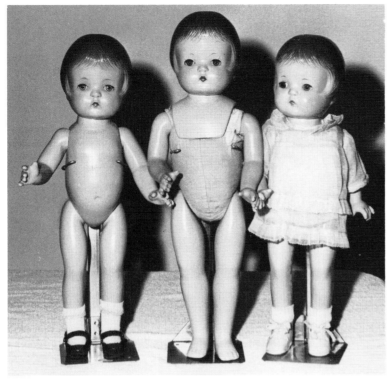

350

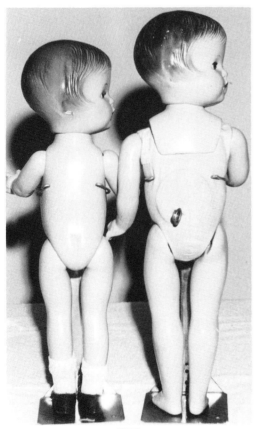

351

352

Illustration 350. Comparative view of an all-composition *Patsy Joan*; the special version of the musical *Patsy Joan* with the shoulder plate, cloth torso and music box; and a dressed *Patsy Joan* with reddish-brown painted hair, brown glassene eyes and wearing a pink organdy handmade dress. Doll in the center, *Esther Farmer Collection.*

Illustration 351. Comparative view of the back of the all-composition *Patsy Joan* and the musical *Patsy Joan*, both seen on the left in *Illustration 350*. Doll on the right, *Esther Farmer Collection.*

Illustration 352. 17½in (45cm) musical *Patsy Joan* variant from 1940, seen in *Illustrations 350* and *351*, wearing her original blue and white cotton dress with trim and buttons. *Esther Farmer Collection.*

Illustration 353. Two *Patsy Joans*. The doll on the left is all-original in her red and white polka dot dress and is wearing red shoes from the late 1930s. Her hair is painted. The doll on the right has her original mohair wig. The inside crown of the original wigs were not completely circular but had two corners designed to cover the front side wisp of molded painted hair on each cheek. However, as soon as the doll was played with a bit, these wisps managed to peek through.

Illustration 354. Side view of the *Patsy Joan*, seen on the right in *Illustration 353*. Wigs were added in 1932 to create something "new and different" but this also created problems. The molded shingled bob was hard to cover up. This doll had been prepared for molded painted hair which was partially removed to affix the newer wig.

353

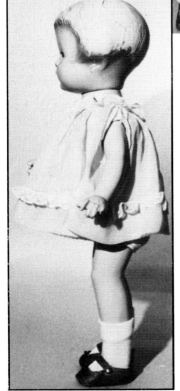

354

Illustration 355. This doll was issued as *Patricia Joan*, but marked "Patsy Joan." She was so named to differentiate human hair wigged dolls from the mohair wigged models. She has a blonde human hair wig, green eyes and wears a green silk Effanbee party dress. *Nancy Carlson Collection. Photograph by David Carlson.*

356

355

Illustration 356. Close-up of the *Patricia Joan*, seen in *Illustration 355*. The human hair wig was apparently considered more deluxe than the mohair wigs and was an effort to keep presenting something "new." There were six sizes of the *Patricia* family with human hair wigs. They were extensively advertised although not illustrated. *Nancy Carlson Collection. Photograph by David Carlson.*

Illustration 357. 16in (41cm) mystery tousle head doll with brown eyes, actually marked "Betty Brite" on a presumed *Patsy Joan* torso. Whether this *Lovums* type head actually came on this body cannot be determined until additional examples are discovered for comparison. *M. Gardner Collection. Photograph by M. Gardner.*

Illustration 358. Back view of the 16in (41cm) mystery tousle head doll, presumably a *Patsy Joan* variant, seen in *Illustration 357*, showing the actual mark on the back of the torso: "EFFanBEE//BETTY BRITE." *M. Gardner Collection. Photography by M. Gardner.*

Illustration 359. Close-up of the marking on the torso of the 16in (41cm) mystery tousle head doll, presumably a *Patsy Joan* variant, seen in *Illustrations 357* and *358*, which reads: "EFFanBEE//BETTY BRITE." *M. Gardner Collection. Photograph by M. Gardner.*

359

360

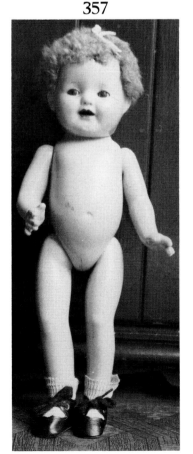

357

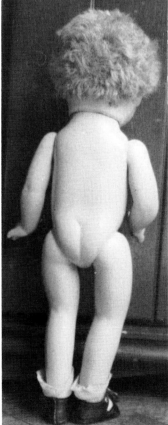

358

Illustration 360. 16in (41cm) mystery tousle head doll, presumably a *Patsy Joan* variant, seen in *Illustrations 357* and *358*, wearing her yellow batiste dress with white lace trim. *M. Gardner Collection. Photograph by M. Gardner.*

361

Illustration 361. 16in (41cm) all-original tousle head *Betty Brite*, a *Patsy Joan* variant, with a gold paper heart-shaped tag pinned to her dress skirt which reads: "This is//BETTY BRITE//TRADE MARK PAT. PEND//The Lovable Imp//with tiltable head//and movable limb//AN// EFFanBEE//DOLL." She is wearing unusual two-toned oxford shoes. Her head is marked: "MARY-LEE," her body is marked: "EFFanBEE//PATSY-JOAN." She has the *Patsy Joan* torso and limbs. *Wilma Moot Collection. Photograph by Barbara Schletzbaum.*

362

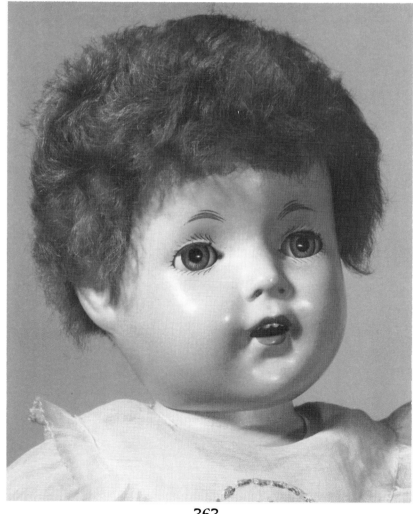

363

Illustration 362. 16in (41cm) all-original tousle head *Betty Brite*, a *Patsy Joan* variant. Her head is marked: "MARY-LEE," her body is marked: "EFFanBEE//PATSY-JOAN." Her gold paper heart-shaped tag proclaims yet a third identity, that of the intended one, *Betty Brite*. She is wearing a pink organdy dress with a white ruffle edged in pink with hand-embroidered touches on the collar and skirt. Her shoes are replaced. *Nancy Carlson Collection. Photograph by David Carlson.*

Illustration 363. Close-up of the 16in (41cm) all-original tousle head *Betty Brite*, a *Patsy Joan* variant, seen in *Illustration 362*. Note her multi-stroked brown eyebrows, her green glassene eyes, her painted upper and lower eyelashes with real hair upper eyelashes also and her open mouth with four upper teeth. Her pink organdy dress has touches of pink and green embroidery on the yoke. *Nancy Carlson Collection. Photograph by David Carlson.*

366

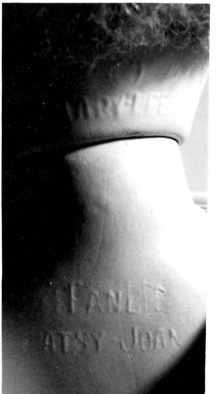

364

365

Illustration 364. Close-up of the marking on the back of the neck and the torso of the 16in (41cm) all-original tousle head *Betty Brite*, a *Patsy Joan* variant, seen in *Illustrations 362* and *363*, which reads, on the neck: "MARY-LEE" and on the torso: "EFFanBEE//PATSY-JOAN." *Nancy Carlson Collection. Photograph by David Carlson.*

Illustration 365. Close-up of the gold paper heart-shaped tag for the 16in (41cm) all-original tousle head *Betty Brite*, a *Patsy Joan* variant, seen in *Illustrations 362* and *363*, which reads: "This is//BETTY BRITE//TRADE MARK PAT. PEND.//The Lovable Imp//with tiltable head//and movable limb//AN//EFFanBEE//DOLL." The doll's head is marked "MARY-LEE," the torso is marked "PATSY-JOAN" and the tag, which is marked "BETTY BRITE," gives her yet another "new" identity. *Nancy Carlson Collection. Photograph by David Carlson.*

Illustration 366. Three of Effanbee's 1946 revived *Patsy Joans*, redesigned with different hairdos, real hair upper eyelashes and painted lower eyelashes. From left to right they are wearing a pink party dress, a multi-colored play dress and a red and white striped party outfit. *Photograph, John Axe Collection.*

367

427—Patsy Joan: 17″ doll. Movable eyes and eyelashes. Movable arms, legs and head. Attractively dressed in peasant style costume, colorfully trimmed. Large bow in back of dress. Bonnet to match. Shoes and socks. 1 doz. to carton.

417 — Patsy Joan: 17″ doll. Striped muslin dress, embroidered collar—puffed sleeves. Matching bonnet with embroidered trim. Movable eyes and eyelashes. Moving arms, legs and head. Shoes, socks. 1 doz. to carton.

427W — Patsy Joan: 17″ doll. Movable eyes and eyelashes. Movable arms, legs and head. Attractively dressed in peasant style costume, colorfully trimmed. Large bow in back of dress. Bonnet to match. Attractive wig. Shoes and socks. 1 doz. to carton.

457W—Patsy Joan: 17″ doll. Organdy dress, petticoat and panties. Dress is trimmed with braid and has puffed sleeves. Matching hat with braid trim. Movable eyes and eyelashes. Movable arms, legs and head. Shoes, socks. Attractive wig. 1 doz. to carton.

487—Colored Patsy Joan: 17″ full composition doll. Moving eyes and eyelashes. Movable arms, legs and head. Smart looking dotted red dress with white yoke. Matching bonnet. Shoes, socks. 1 doz. to carton.

368

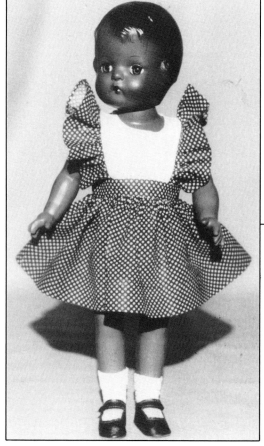

369

Illustration 367. Original advertisement from an unknown Seattle, Washington, newspaper for December 12, 1946, for *Patsy Joan* in a red felt coat and bonnet with a shoulder strap purse for $4.95.

Illustration 368. Page from the catalog entitled "Effanbee Dolls for 1949" showing the redesigned *Patsy Joan* in five different costumes and with the gold paper heart-shaped tag. The doll itself is marked "EFFANDBEE [with a "D" added]" on the back. Note that doll number 487 is for a black version, here called "colored," in a red dress with a white yoke.

Illustration 369. 17in (43cm) all-original black *Patsy Joan*. This is the version that is seen in *Illustration 368* on the right. *Private Collection.*

371

Illustration 370. 17in (43cm) black *Patsy Joan*. This is the version shown in *Illustration 369* on the right. Her gold metal heart-shaped bracelet tag has been added as she came with a gold paper heart-shaped tag. *Inge Simms Collection.*

Illustration 371. Close-up of the 17in (43cm) black *Patsy Joan*, seen in *Illustration 370*. She has brown eyes, real hair upper eyelashes and painted lower eyelashes. *Inge Simms Collection.*

Illustration 372. 17in (43cm) black *Patsy Joan*, seen in *Illustrations 370* and *371*, shown undressed. The body contour of the 1946 to 1949 *Patsy Joan* was more of an adult type torso such as most girl dolls had after the introduction of the *Shirley Temple* doll in 1934. *Inge Simms Collection.*

372

370

Illustration 373. 17in (43cm) *Patsy Joan* dolls *from 1946.* The black doll on the left is all original with its gold paper heart-shaped tag. The doll on the right has replaced shoes and socks. *Linda Den Boer Collection. Photograph by Linda Den Boer.*

Illustration 374. Side view of the 17in (43cm) *Patsy Joan* dolls, seen in *Illustrations 373.* The black version is much sought-after but the white version is more easily located. *Linda Den Boer Collection. Photograph by Linda Den Boer.*

Illustration 375. Original advertisement from the Sears, Roebuck and Co. 1950 Christmas catalog showing an example of a **known** named doll not identified by name in the catalog. *Patsy Joan* is listed as "Outdoor Girl" here.

373

374

Big value Girl Dolls

[E] **Outdoor girl** . . . dressed to frolic in the sun. Wears cotton play dress (asst'd styles), matching bonnet with wide brim, ribbon tie. Rayon socks, imitation leather shoes. Composition body; tinted hair. Jointed arms, legs . . . head turns, tilts. Sleeping glass eyes with real lashes.
49 N 3548—Shipping weight 2 lbs.. . .$2.98

$2.98
16½-in. doll

[E] $2.98

375

Chapter Nine

Patsy Lou,

Big Sister

Regrettably for a researcher, *Patsy Lou,* such a big important doll in her day, did not have a page of advertising to herself in the trade magazines as did some of her earlier sisters. The depressed economic climate may have had something to do with this.

She was listed over *Patsy Ann, Patsy Joan, Patsykin* and *Patsyette* as early as May 1931 with no illustrations. One wonders if the company could have listed her before she was actually available since she is not included in the F.A.O. Schwarz 1931 Christmas catalog.

At least some of the *Patsy Lou* dolls had personalized gold metal heart-shaped bracelet tags. The gold paper heart-shaped tag was the same as *Patsy Ann's* only with *Patsy Lou's* name imprinted on it. She is featured in the F.A.O. Schwarz 1932 Christmas catalog. The description reads: "Such a lovable Imp, with tiltable head and movable limbs — Patsy Lou — the largest of the Adorable Patsy dolls, measuring 22" tall. Smartly modelled bob and long lashed movable eyes, a charming pink figured, puff sleeved dress with white organdie collar and a cunning ribbon trimmed pocket on her skirt. Her sunbonnet matches the dress. She wears white shoes and stockings. Patsy Lou, like her sisters, is made of almost unbreakable composition." She was available for $8.00. There was no trunk trousseau as yet for her as there was for *Patsy, Patsy Joan* and *Patsy Ann.*

The doll at this time was still intended to portray a quite young child. Oftentimes in re-dressing, the dolls have turned out looking much older than originally intended. One could buy separately from F.A.O. Schwarz a four-piece outdoor set consisting of a flannel coat trimmed with krimmer, zippered leggings and a hat and muff in red or green, for $3.75.

There were other outfits available also. A riding habit consisting of a flannel coat, breeches and a hat, leatherette leggings in red or tan and a white shirt with a silk tie sold for $3.25. A rain set consisting of a coat, hat and umbrella, in green, tan or red, sold for $3.00. A flannel bathrobe in pink or blue was available for $1.25. A fur coat with a beret to match, in white only, cost $7.50. This deluxe outfit cost nearly the same as the entire doll. Effanbee also issued some of its own models of fur coats.

The wigged versions of *Patsy Lou* had a somewhat older look. This version was first shown in *Playthings* magazine with the NRA (National Recovery Administration) symbol (of an eagle) saying that she would be featured in *The Patsytown News,* sent out to thousands of little girls. (The National Industrial Recovery Act was passed by Congress in 1933 and administered by the National Recovery Administration following the stock market crash of 1929 and the economic depression.) *Patsy Lou's* wig is topped by a large hair bow, which was quite different from the earlier bandeau. The dolls with molded hair were also available.

Although the Ideal Novelty and Toy Company received the rights to make the *Shirley Temple* doll, Effanbee had the extreme good fortune to have the little actress associate with its dolls. In some of her first publicity for 20th Century Fox studios, Shirley posed with a wigged *Patsy Lou* wearing riding jodhpurs. (This outfit may have been created in the F.A.O.

Schwarz studios and is very rare.) Shirley wears the polka dot dancing dress from her sensational 1934 appearance in *Stand Up and Cheer*. *Patsy Lou* had a featured part in the movie *Bright Eyes* as a Christmas gift to Shirley, while Jane Withers, also in the movie, received an elaborate Lenci doll. The latter doll actually became part of Shirley's doll collection after the completion of the movie.

A publicity bonanza for Effanbee came in 1933 when First Lady Eleanor Roosevelt allowed herself to be photographed by Hearst Metrotone News as she was shopping for toys for her grandchildren. The *New York Herald* newspaper ran a rotogravure photograph by Acme of Mrs. Roosevelt with Santa and a young saleslady. Two *Patsy Lous* are shown in the foreground in polka dot jumper dresses with brimmed hats to match.

By February of 1934, *Playthings* magazine printed a photograph of Mrs. Roosevelt holding *Patsy Lou* for the camera. The gold metal heart-shaped bracelet tag and the gold paper heart-shaped tag are visible on the arms. The message with the photograph said that Mrs. Roosevelt was purchasing *Patsy Lou*. The caption to the short news story read: "Patsy Lou in the White House." The text read: "All of the Patsy dolls made by Fleischaker and Baum are favorites with the children of America, but just now Patsy Lou is high-hatting all the other Patsys. Believe it or not, Patsy Lou has actually had her picture taken with Mrs. Roosevelt and just to show that she's telling the truth, she has sent a copy of the photograph to Playthings. Patsy Lou is certainly a very proud and happy young lady." No doubt Mrs. Roosevelt's granddaughter, "Sistie" Dahl, was to become the new owner of the *Patsy Lou*.

In 1934, Effanbee gave the Whitman Publishing Company of Racine, Wisconsin, permission to reproduce a paper doll book, 11in (28cm) by 17½ in (45cm), using a photographic copy of a *Patsy Lou* doll on the front cover and *Barbara Lou* on the back cover with garments for each. A golden heart-shaped symbol on the cover reads: "This is a//Reproduction of the//GEUNINE//EFFANBEE//DOLL." Beneath that it reads: "Through The Courtesy of//The Manufacturers of//Genuine EFF AN BEE DOLLS.//#976." *Patsy Lou* is shown with blonde curls which reach not quite to the shoulders, blue eyes with eyelashes and a small rosebud mouth. Someone has substituted her own one-piece combination undergarment which she came with for *Barbara Lou's* short ruffled panties. They do not fit well on her fat tummy, yet the idea may have been to show more of her composition body. Four outfits are photographed for *Patsy Lou* and four for *Barbara Lou*, one of Effanbee's *American Children*.

Since there seems to be so little catalog documentation of *Patsy Lou*, the contemporary photographs of her in original outfits in the Whitman paper doll book help greatly to document how she looked in original garments, even though the paper doll book was issued in 1939 and the doll and garments are circa 1936.

Illustration 376. Original advertisement from the F.A.O. Schwarz 1932 Christmas catalog for the 22in (56cm) *Patsy Lou*. She is shown wearing a pink figured puff-sleeved dress with a hand-embroidered white organdy collar and was available for $8.00.

Illustration 377. The marking on the torso of the *Patsy Lou* dolls which reads: "EFFanBEE//'PATSY LOU'." There was no marking on the head.

Illustration 378. The personalized gold metal heart-shaped bracelet tag which came on at least some of the *Patsy Lou* dolls. It reads: "EFFanBEE//PATSY//LOU."

PATSY LOU

No. A-643—Such a lovable Imp, with tiltable head and movable limbs—Patsy Lou—the largest of the Adorable Patsy dolls, measuring 22" tall. Smartly modelled bob and long lashed movable eyes, a charming pink figured, puff sleeved dress with white organdie collar and a cunning ribbon trimmed pocket on her skirt. Her sunbonnet matches the dress. She wears white shoes and stockings. Patsy Lou, like her sisters, is made of almost unbreakable composition............**$8.00**

376

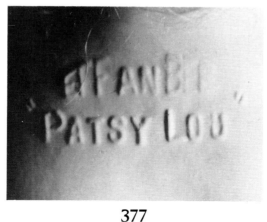

377

378

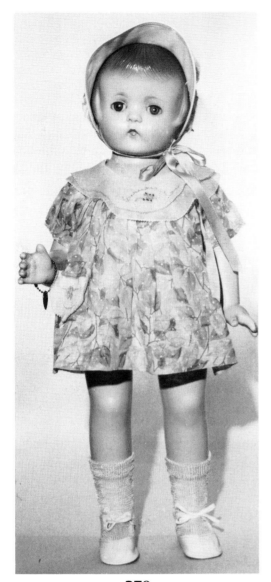

380

Illustration 382. Back view of the 22in (56cm) *Patsy Lou*, seen in *Illustration 381*, showing the detail of her shingled hairdo, the placement of the woven tag at the waist of the dress and a close-up of the actual label in the lower left-hand corner.

379

Illustration 379. 22in (56cm) *Patsy Lou* in her original Effanbee style dress. This is the same outfit that was offered on the *Patsy Lou* shown in the advertisement from F.A.O. Schwarz as seen in *Illustration 376*. She is wearing a sheer dotted cotton dress in shades of blue and white with a white organdy hand-embroidered double collar and a ribbon-trimmed piqué pocket, a flowered bonnet with a white piqué brim and her shoes have been replaced. She dates from 1932.

Illustration 380. Side view of the 22in (56cm) *Patsy Lou*, seen in *Illustration 379*, showing the detail of the bonnet and the double collar.

Illustration 381. 22in (56cm) *Patsy Lou*; molded painted hair; wears a blue and white polka dot batiste Effanbee style dress with a pearl button embroidered into the collar trim, bonnet is missing, shoes are replaced; dress has the woven Effanbee label with the gold heart and the red lettering, sewn into the waist, which reads: "EFFanBEE//DURABLE//DOLLS [within the heart]" and underneath "MADE IN U.S.A." She dates from 1933.

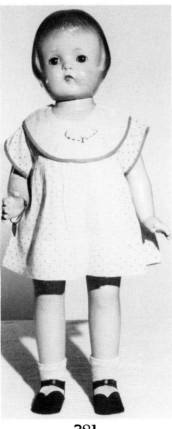

381

382

Illustration 383. 22in (56cm) *Patsy Lou;* molded painted hair; brown glassene eyes, real hair upper eyelashes, painted upper and lower eyelashes, a rosebud mouth; wears a red and white polka dot dress and bonnet made from a McCall pattern. The shoes are replacements. The costume was created by the author's mother, Mrs. Hilda Bewley.

Illustration 384. Close-up of the 22in (56cm) *Patsy Lou,* seen in *Illustration 383.* Note the detail of the eyes and the modeling of the hair.

Illustration 385. 22in (56cm) *Patsy Lou,* seen in *Illustrations 383* and *384,* showing the detail of the bonnet.

In 1934, *The Patsytown News* lists, in addition to *Patsy Lou,* a *Patsy Alice* as being 26in (66cm) tall. This will come as a surprise to collectors who felt they had a complete set of this family group.

It is believed that this doll had a different body and legs but with the same head as was used on *Patsy Lou.* If there was a doll actually marked "Patsy Alice," surely one would have surfaced by now. It was suggested that she might be a variant with a cloth body and a separate composition shoulder head, but the company clearly always listed dolls in columns, with all of one type together as with the all-composition ones.

Since beginning this study, the author has had the opportunity to examine dolls she is convinced were those described as *Patsy Alice.* The doll has a human hair wig with a head mold identical to that of *Patsy Lou* and identically sized arms. The composition torso has been lengthened out and is completely unmarked, yet unquestionably an all-original product. The legs are a bit longer and slimmer than those of *Patsy Lou,* adding up to 26in (66cm). We are anticipating the future discovery of one of these scarce 26in (66cm) dolls in its original clothing with a gold paper heart-shaped tag on the arm to positively identify it as *Patsy Alice.*

The uncovering of mysteries is one facet of the hobby that keeps it tantalizing and fascinating. It would not be nearly as exciting if all the mysteries were solved. Yet we try to fit back as many of the pieces of the puzzle as possible. You the reader/collector can help by participating about any Effanbee doll. They are doll history which would be lost in the future without documentation.

383

385

384

388

386

387

Illustration 388. 22in (56cm) *Patsy Lou*; reddish-brown painted hair; brown glassene eyes; wears her original yellow and pale green sweater, yellow wool pleated skirt, replaced shoes. This doll has the rare celluloid inset fingernails. *Dorothy Tonkin Collection. Photograph by David Carlson.*

Illustration 386. The advertisement in the September 1933 issue of *Toys and Novelties* magazine declared "Now Patsys Have Hair. Striking Improvement in the Famous PATSY Family. Stylish Personality wigs now grace the head of all the Patsy Dolls, accenting the beauty of this quick selling family." In the same advertisement, *The Patsytown News* was said to be new. At this time the dolls carried the NRA (National Recovery Administration) label, as shown to the side.

Illustration 387. 22in (56cm) *Patsy Lou* models a specialty shop dress and bonnet with no label. The dress is flowered organdy with pink roses and buds, white ruffles on the dress and the cap and pink ribbon trim. The shoes and socks are replaced.

Illustration 389. 22in (56cm) *Patsy Lou*; blonde human hair "personality" wig; brown glassene eyes; wears all-original white dress with pink hemstitching on the skirt ruffle, wine-colored ribbon on the dress, socks with stripes. The label on the front of the skirt refers to the human hair wig. *Marilyn Ankenbauer Collection. Photograph by Marilyn Ankenbauer.*

Illustration 390. 22in (56cm) *Patsy Lou*; blonde mohair wig; brown glassene eyes; wears a navy blue cotton sailor dress with matching combination undergarments, replaced shoes and socks. *Bothwell/Chapman Collection. Photograph by owner.*

389

390

Illustration 391. Close-up of the 22in (56cm) *Patsy Lou*, seen in *Illustration 390*, showing the detail of the face. *Bothwell/Chapman Collection. Photograph by owner.*

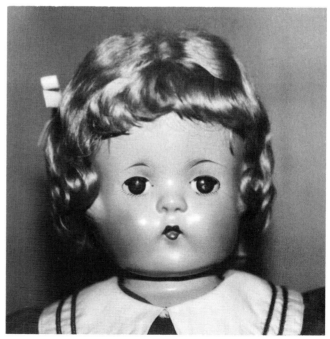

391

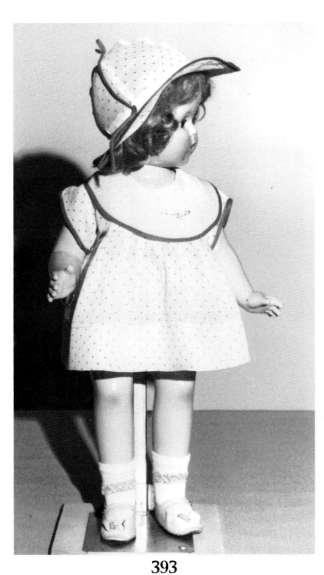

393

Illustration 392. 22in (56cm) *Patsy Lou*; blonde mohair wig; blue glassene eyes; wears a polka dotted swiss dress with a deep white collar bound in blue bias tape as are the bonnet and the sleeves, socks with blue patterned stripes. She dates from 1933.

392

396

394

395

Illustration 394. Comparative view of two 22in (56cm) *Patsy Lous*. *Patsy Lou* on the left has a red mohair wig and wears a yellow party dress. *Patsy Lou* on the right has reddish painted hair and wears her original sweater with a pleated skirt. This is the same doll seen in *Illustration 388*. Doll on the left, *Nancy Carlson Collection*. Doll on the right, *Dorothy Tonkin Collection*. *Photograph by David Carlson*.

Illustration 395. 22in (56cm) *Patsy Lou*, seen on the left in *Illustration 394*; red mohair wig; blue-gray glassene eyes; wears her all-original yellow organdy ensemble. The collar ruffle and accordion pleated skirt style were similar to the *Shirley Temple* doll's dancing dress. *Nancy Carlson Collection*. *Photograph by David Carlson*.

Illustration 396. Close-up of the back of the 22in (56cm) *Patsy Lou*, seen in *Illustrations 394* and *395*, showing the marking on the torso: "EFFanBEE//'PATSY LOU'." *Nancy Carlson Collection*. *Photograph by David Carlson*.

In Washington

The President's wife getting assistance from Santa Claus as she finished her shopping for toys for her grandchildren.

Herald Tribune—Acme

397

Illustration 397. On December 24, 1933, the *New York Herald* newspaper printed this photograph of First Lady Eleanor Roosevelt shopping for toys for her grandchildren. Two *Patsy Lous* are shown in the foreground in polka dot jumper dresses with matching brimmed hats. The dolls at this time carried the NRA (National Recovery Administration) labels. The National Industrial Recovery Act, which was passed by Congress in 1933 and administered by the National Recovery Administration, was instigated by President Roosevelt.

Illustration 398. In the February 1934 issue of *Playthings* magazine, a photograph of First Lady Eleanor Roosevelt is shown as she was shopping before Christmas in 1933. She is holding a *Patsy Lou* which she chose for her granddaughter.

398

Illustration 399. Publicity shot of Shirley Temple for the 1934 film *Bright Eyes*. Here Shirley is imitating *Patsy Lou's* solemn expression.

Illustration 400. Another publicity shot of Shirley Temple for the 1934 movie *Bright Eyes* with a *Patsy Lou* doll.

400

399

Illustration 401. Yet another publicity shot of Shirley Temple for the 1934 film *Bright Eyes*. The *Patsy Lou* doll Shirley is holding is a Christmas gift to her from her screen mother.

Illustration 402. In this publicity shot of Shirley Temple holding her *Patsy Lou*, for the 1934 movie *Bright Eyes*, the gold metal heart-shaped bracelet tag can be seen on *Patsy Lou's* wrist. This doll has a mohair wig in its original set, metal eyes and wears an organdy dress and bonnet.

401

402

Illustration 403. 22in (56cm) all-original *Patsy Lou*; auburn wig in its original set; wears an organdy dress with touches of embroidery on the collar and a bonnet. This is the same type of doll used in the 1934 movie *Bright Eyes*. *Sue Brownell Collection. Photograph by Sue Brownell.*

Illustration 404. In 1934, Shirley Temple, wearing her costume from the movie *Stand Up and Cheer*, posed proudly with a *Patsy Lou* doll.

Illustration 405. *Patsy Lou*, from the Whitman paper doll book, models a crisp blue organdy dress with a high waistline and a deep collar ruffle which has a picoted edge. A row of hemstitching trims the skirt followed by a ruffle and then another row of hemstitching, finished off by a picoted ruffle at the bottom. This outfit was said to be suitable for dancing school or a party.

404

403

405

406

408

407

Illustration 406. Contemporary photograph of a blonde 22in (56cm) *Patsy Lou*, from the Whitman paper doll book, circa 1936. She is wearing a medium blue pleated dress shown in color in a paper doll book, with a white collar trimmed in soutache braid. The garment is described as suitable for school.

Illustration 407. Contemporary photograph of *Patsy Lou* from the paper doll book by the Whitman Publishing Company. She is wearing a blue woolen suit and tam-o'-shanter which are said to be suitable to wear to go calling on friends. The jacket is red, blue, yellow and navy plaid with light blue binding at the neck, jacket bottom and sleeves. It has light blue covered buttons. She dates from circa 1936.

Illustration 408. *Patsy Lou*, from the Whitman paper doll book, models a crisp pink percale print dress with outline hand-stitching on the collar. The belt appears to be leatherette with a buckle. (Not too many natural waistline outfits were used on the "fat torso" dolls.) There are three rows of red braid trim on the skirt.

Illustration 409. Advertisement from an unknown newspaper for October 30, 1934, for the Meier & Frank Co. in Portland, Oregon, about its 32nd annual doll show. There were 20 competition classes for children to enter their dolls in, with prizes of nearly $300 in cash and merchandise. Every child contestant would receive a gift, winner or not. A wigged *Patsy Lou* carries the banner. Artwork on the arm enables it to hold the banner. A *Mary Ann* by Effanbee appears to be next in line. What a happy way to advertise the new dolls for Christmas!

Illustration 410. Original advertisement from an unknown December 10, 1933, newspaper for *Patsy* dolls. It actually includes other Effanbee dolls sold by E. M. Kahn & Co. in the Toy Shop. Note the doll in the back row which uses the *Patsy Ann* torso and fur wig which is simply named *Tousle Head*. Very large mama dolls are called *Big Girl* dolls here.

410

214

411

412

413

Illustration 411. Original advertisement for *Patsy Lou* from the *American Toy Pictorial* for 1936. This was part of a full-page advertisement for *Dy-Dee Baby, Patricia, Sugar* and the movie *Anne Shirley* doll. The *Anne Shirley* doll, a country child, wore gingham and T-strap sandals, so the *Patsys* wore their own version in 1936. *Patsy Lou's* wig is longer and less curly and her dress is longer. She wears both the gold metal heart-shaped bracelet tag and the gold paper heart-shaped tag. Note that she has "painted" fingernails.

Illustration 412. 22in (56cm) *Patsy Lou* variant which came as a *Tousle Head* version but also with a human hair wig. She has the typical *Patsy Lou* body which is marked "EFFanBEE//'PATSY LOU'" and uses the *Lovums* head with blue-gray eyes and an open mouth with two upper and two lower teeth. This doll is much more difficult to locate than the 19in (48cm) *Patsy Ann* variant. This version is mentioned in *The Patsytown News*.

Illustration 413. 23in (58cm) *Patsy Lou* variant using the *Patsy Lou* head with a thick blonde human hair wig and a separate shoulder piece. Her complete composition arms are jointed and the composition legs to above the knees can be made to simulate walking by a child. This is a latter day mama doll with a cryer. To date no similar all-original doll with tags or labels has been located. *Gerrie Lee Collection.*

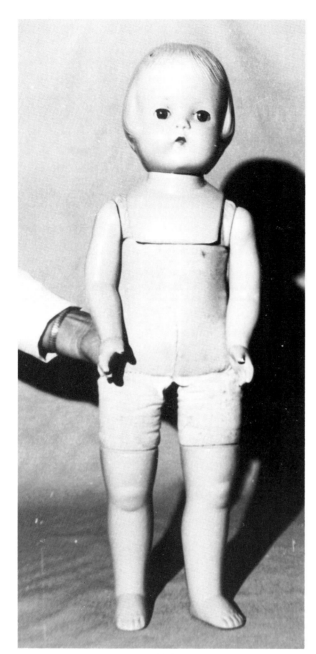

414

Illustration 414. 22in (56cm) *Patsy Lou* variant with a *Patsy Lou* head on a *Lovums* shoulder plate, cloth mama doll body with a voice and swing legs, full composition arms, composition legs to above the knees; brown eyes with real hair eyelashes.

Illustration 415. 22in (56cm) *Patsy Lou* variant, seen in *Illustration 414*, shown with her head turned.

415

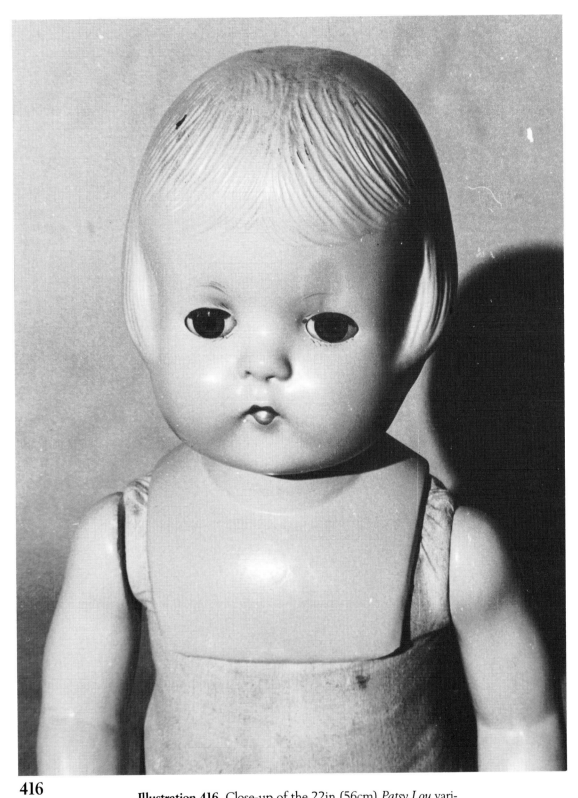

416

Illustration 416. Close-up of the 22in (56cm) *Patsy Lou* variant, seen in *Illustrations 414* and *415*, showing the detail of the face and the neck and shoulder plate.

417

Illustration 417. 26in (66cm) all-original *Patsy Lou* variant; composition head, shoulder plate, arms and legs, cloth body; luxurious blonde human hair wig on her *Patsy Lou* head; wears cotton multi-colored floral bouquet patterned dress with a fitted waistline, tucking on the puffed sleeves, high yoke with separate suspender effect, original socks and side-snap shoes; wears her gold metal heart-shaped bracelet tag which reads: "EFFANBEE//DURABLE//DOLL." *Private Collection.*

418

Illustration 418. 26in (66cm) all-original *Patsy Lou* variant, seen in *Illustration 417*, shown wearing her white cotton slip with a fitted waistline. *Private Collection*.

Illustration 419. 26in (66cm) all-original *Patsy Lou* variant, seen in *Illustrations 417* and *418*, shown undressed. Note the slimmer shaped torso. To date, an all-original example with a name tag has not been located. *Private Collection*.

419

McCALL
PRINTED PATTERN

Dolls Outfit with Transfer Size 22

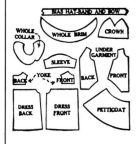

BIAS HAT-BAND AND BOW

WHOLE COLLAR · WHOLE BRIM · CROWN

UNDER GARMENT

SLEEVE

BACK · YOKE · FRONT · BACK · FRONT

DRESS BACK · DRESS FRONT · PETTICOAT

Dress & Hat
(Size 22 Inches)
Material Required

32 or 35 Inch Material	⅝ yd.
39 " "	½ "
Contrasting	
32 or 39 Inch Material	⅜ "
Crinoline for Brim	
35 Inch Material..........	⅜ "
Under Garment	
32 or 35 Inch Material	⅓ "
Lace Edging (¾ Inch).....	2½ "

12 Pieces and 1 Transfer

The Pattern with the Printed Cutting Line

This pattern includes PRINTO GRAVURE

Cutting diagrams for laying this size on several widths of material

Construction diagrams showing how to assemble

Finishing details

Cut through the white center of the double cutting lines. Sew on broken lines.

Traduction Francaise sur le patron

La Traduccion en Espanol en el patron

Made in U. S. A.

Illustration 420. Front cover of a sample McCall pattern for the 22in (56cm) *Patsy Lou*. This was copyright in 1933 and given away by The McCall Co. as a promotion. The envelope measures 3in (8cm) by 4in (10cm).

Illustration 421. Back cover of the sample McCall pattern, shown in *Illustration 420*.

Index